THE POWER OF RECOVERY

VOICES OF STRENGTH, RESILIENCE, AND CHANGE

Co-authored and Compiled by
Patrick McElwaine, PsyD

The Power of Recovery: Voices of Strength, Resilience, and Change
© 2026 Patrick McElwaine, PsyD

Editing, formatting, and design by Let's Get Booked

ISBN: 979-8-9954841-0-3

FOR EVERYONE IMPACTED BY ADDICTION

For those who suffer in silence.
For those who have found their voice.
For the ones in active recovery—
and the ones still searching for hope.

For families holding on,
and friends who don't know what to say
but stay anyway.

This book is for you.

We hope these stories shine a light into the shadows,
offering comfort, connection, and courage.

May you find strength in these pages,
and leave with your heart a little fuller,
your mind a little clearer,
and your spirit reminded:

You are not alone.

YOU ARE NOT ALONE

This book is for anyone whose life has been touched by addiction.

It's for the person struggling to get through another day without using—and wondering if recovery is even possible.

It's for the person in active recovery, working to rebuild their life one step, one day, one breath at a time.

It's for the friend, parent, sibling, or partner who loves someone battling addiction and is searching for answers, support, or simply a sign that they're not alone.

It's for students, therapists, counselors, and anyone who wants to better understand addiction—not just as a diagnosis, but as a human experience full of pain, complexity, resilience, and possibility.

It's for people who believe in second chances, who know what it means to fall and get back up, and who want to hold space for both the heartbreak and the healing.

Whether you are here to learn, to feel seen, or to offer support, we hope these stories remind you that recovery is real, hope is powerful, and no one is ever too far gone to change.

FOR YOUR ATTENTION:

This book contains stories that are raw, courageous, and deeply human. They reflect the reality of addiction, recovery, and healing—and may evoke strong emotional responses.

While we believe in the power of sharing lived experiences, we also recognize that some content may trigger readers. Please take care of yourself as you engage with these pages.

Topics Covered in This Book Include:

Addiction and Mental Health
- Substance Use and Addiction
- Alcoholism and Drug Dependence
- Relapses and Recovery
- Mental Illness
- PTSD and Complex Trauma
- Recovery from Co-Occurring Disorders

Trauma and Abuse
- Childhood Trauma
- Childhood Sexual Abuse
- Sexual Assault
- Intimate Partner Violence
- Domestic Violence

Grief, Loss, and Suicide
- Death and Grief (including loss of a parent, child, or spouse)
- Suicide and Suicidal Ideation
- Self-Harm

Life Challenges and Identity
- Divorce and Relationship Loss

- Parenting in Recovery
- Foster Care and Adoption
- Incarceration
- Immigration and Identity
- Homelessness
- Bullying and Social Isolation

Emotional and Relational Themes
- Eating Disorders
- Codependency
- Stigma and Shame
- Faith, Spirituality, and Crisis of Belief

These topics are included because they are part of real human experiences—and because healing requires honesty. If you need support, please know that help is available. You are not alone.

Resource List

You'll find a comprehensive resource list at the back of this book (starting on page 183) to support individuals at every stage of the recovery journey—whether you're:
- Currently struggling with addiction
- Supporting a loved one
- Actively working on your own recovery
- Or simply curious about what recovery looks like

This Section Includes:

- **Crisis and Helpline Numbers** – Immediate support in urgent or life-threatening situations
- **National and Local Organizations** – Including SAMHSA, NAMI, and others offering advocacy and education.

- **12-Step and Mutual Support Groups** – AA, NA, Al-Anon, SMART Recovery, and more
- **Therapeutic Resources** – How to find a therapist, trauma-informed care, and specialty providers.
- **Digital Tools and Apps** – Tools for sobriety tracking, crisis planning, mindfulness, and more.
- **Books, Podcasts, and Articles** – Recommended readings and audio content to inform and uplift.
- **Family and Loved One Support** – Boundaries, self-care, and support for those affected by addiction.

Whether you're taking your first step, continuing your healing, or trying to understand someone else's journey, this book and these resources are here to support you.

You are not alone. Help is available, and healing is possible.

TABLE OF CONTENTS

ACKNOWLEDGMENTS

I am deeply grateful to the Ray and Mildred Taylor Award program for its generous support, which made this book possible. This award was established through an endowment created by Carol Taylor H'22, RN, Ph.D.—a former Holy Family University faculty member who served in the School of Nursing & Health Sciences from 1979–1987 and 1995–1997. Carol and her family created the award in honor of her parents, Ray and Mildred Taylor. Carol's distinguished contributions were recognized by the School of Nursing & Health Sciences with the Distinguished Nursing Alumni Award in October 2012, and she was honored with a Doctor of Humane Letters, *honoris causa*, at Holy Family University's 2022 Commencement. The Ray and Mildred Taylor Awards support faculty who have completed at least two years of full-time teaching at Holy Family, with priority given to proposals that advance faculty research and scholarship. I am honored to have been selected as a recipient and sincerely appreciate the vital role this award played in the development of this book

I would also like to express my heartfelt thanks to Kristie Knights and Unsung Heroes Publishing for their unwavering support and belief in this project. Kristie's guidance, encouragement, and commitment to helping bring important stories to light have meant the world to me. Her compassion and professionalism made this process not only possible but personally meaningful. I am equally grateful to Amanda Horan of Let's Get Booked, whose editorial expertise, patience, and incredible support were truly invaluable. Amanda was amazing to work with and extremely helpful, thoughtful, and deeply invested in strengthening this book every step of the way.

To my wife, Elyse, and my daughters, Morgan and Eva—thank you for being my constant source of love and strength. Your presence in my life gives me purpose and keeps me grounded. And to our dog, Charlie, thank you for always reminding me to take breaks, go for walks, and stay in the moment.

Finally, I am incredibly grateful to the dedicated proofreaders who lent their time and expertise to help shape and polish this manuscript. Their thoughtful insights, attention to detail, and deep care for the content were essential to the final product.

Maria Diaz, who holds a Bachelor of Arts in Psychology and a Master of Science in Counseling Psychology from Holy Family University, is currently pursuing a doctorate in the Psychology and Neuroscience department at Temple University. Her research focuses on adaptive and maladaptive behaviors in emerging adults, including social media use, coping strategies, and substance-related issues. Maria is especially interested in social stressors such as perceived discrimination, and she explores gender and cultural differences in her work.

Gina O'Rourke serves as the Administrative Assistant for the Graduate Counseling Psychology Master's and Doctoral programs at Holy Family University. She was honored to serve as a trusted editor on this project, helping bring each author's authentic voice to life. Growing up in a family impacted by active addiction and alcoholism, Gina is grateful to have chosen a different path. She shares God's grace with her husband, Sean, and their wonderful family. A passionate writer since childhood, Gina has been published in *Folio* magazine and enjoys poetry, group fitness, and stained-glass artistry. She dedicates her work on this book to her mother, who celebrates 21 years of courageous sobriety this year: "Mom, I love you and am so very proud of you."

Jessica Jones Philipbar is a passionate advocate for communication, storytelling, and personal growth. After graduating from Saint Joseph's University and Hofstra Law School, she practiced law before pursuing a master's in counseling psychology to deepen her commitment to mental health. A gifted writer and editor, Jessica believes great writing happens in revision—and that "no sentence is complete until it has survived three rounds of existential doubt." She resides in Yardley, PA, with her husband, Baer, and their dogs, Lucy and Penny.

Sean Pramnieks, a current graduate student in the Counseling Psychology program at Holy Family University, holds a Bachelor of Arts in Psychology and is completing his master's with a focus on outpatient family therapy. He is also involved in research examining the relationship between academic belongingness and social media behavior among university students. Sean hopes to become both a counselor supporting children and families through trauma and an adjunct professor.

Nicole Spirk is a graduate of Moravian University and Wilkes University and currently serves as a fifth-grade teacher at Spring Garden Elementary School in Bethlehem, Pennsylvania. With a deep commitment to education and a careful eye for detail, Nicole generously contributed her time and skills to the final proofreading of this book, helping ensure clarity, consistency, and flow throughout the manuscript. Outside of the classroom, Nicole enjoys spending time with her husband, Matthew Spirk, and their two children, Callie and Colin, along with their two dogs Trixie and Penny. She loves to travel, read, and is also an avid soccer fan who appreciates opportunities to balance her professional life with family, community, and the activities she loves.

FOREWORD
Dr. Stephanie Yoder

How many psychologists do you know who would wear a leprechaun costume to brighten the day of patients in an inpatient psychiatric facility? This was the first thought that popped into my head about "Dr. Mac" when he asked me to write a foreword for this book. I have worked with over one hundred students who are or were training to become clinical psychologists, and although all are dear to me, Patrick McElwaine stands out for several reasons.

Pat is one of the most positive clinicians I have ever had the pleasure of working with. Over time, I have discovered that there is a certain glow of positivity that can be a common variable for those who are not only in recovery but work it into every facet of their lives. This positivity does not come from the ease of being in recovery, but, conversely, from the pain, hard work, and thereby growth that come from that daily, hourly, and sometimes minute-by-minute struggle. In all my time knowing Pat, his positivity has remained a constant throughout his work, including working with people at their lowest points and in the midst of severe psychiatric crises.

Supervising Pat in his early therapeutic career in the psychiatric hospital where I work, I remember giving him the feedback that I thought he was using his "recovery lens" and his experience with recovery from drug and alcohol abuse too much in sessions. In retrospect, this is likely one of Pat's greatest strengths as a psychologist. Psychologists are often seen by the clients or consumers with whom we work as omnipotent, as being the pinnacle of mental health at all times and having a life devoid of problems. While this can be grist for the mill in exploring projections people may put onto us, the reality is that the curative factor in therapy is the relationship. Pat is unique in his extroverted manner in a field predominantly filled with introverts. Pat's ability to meet an individual where they are, demonstrate his "humanness," and instill hope are likely the cornerstones of his success.

It is a testament to Pat that his legend still lives on in the psychiatric hospital where he worked so many years ago. I remember when he told me he was leaving to start his career teaching at his alma mater. I realized what a huge loss this was for our hospital, but I was also incredibly proud of him for stepping out to create an enormous impact in the field of psychology. Upon telling my boss that he was leaving, he said, "Well, find another one, you know, just like Pat." I promptly informed him that it was an impossible task. Pat is one of a kind, atypical in every splendid way. As a result of his wise choice, he has been able to impact the lives of so many clinicians, exponentially spreading his knowledge to those in training so that they too may change people's lives for the better. Today, he is a program director for a master's degree program in counseling psychology, is a faculty member for the prestigious Beck Institute in Philadelphia, and is involved with providing education and support to many different agencies that provide services for those in recovery for drug and alcohol issues as well as mental health issues. He is active with the local NAMI community as well and seems to have endless energy regarding recovery in every sense of the word.

Through reading this book, I am certain that the thread of hope will inspire people to either begin their journey of recovery, bolster their current journey, or further their work in helping others. It is impossible for anything less to occur given the compassion, motivation, and talent found within. The definition of recovery means different things to different people, but it is important to remember that it is an expedition. The learning comes from the work within and along the way and is never a straight line. In fact, the ride more closely resembles a rollercoaster, sometimes up, sometimes down, sometimes hurtling into dizzying spirals. The importance is getting on the ride, holding on for dear life, wearing a seatbelt, and following the conductor's instructions. Like a roller coaster ride, in healing, you in part give your life over to a person you may not know but who has the tools to keep you safe, guide you, tell you when to start, and when to get off. Whether the journey in question is short-term, long-term, or lifelong, this book will hopefully open your mind to it, provide you with hope, and open the door to the questions that will facilitate your own personal quest.

For those in a healing profession, or with an aspiration to do so, find your own path. While Pat is a wonderful role model for being real, yet maintaining his positivity and empathy, one can never be "Pat." A good teacher is the one superseded by their student, the one who gathers the wisdom and spirit of their best teachers and finds their own way to instill those lessons in others. To do so, one must have courage, be genuine, truly believe in people's ability to heal, and do so truthfully with one's own voice, all within the confines of ethical practice and knowledge. Equally important is the healer's own treatment path, which is continual and without an endpoint.

Within the depths of this book, there are lessons for people at any stage of change. Whether just contemplating the possibility of change or working to effectively maintain life-altering changes that have already occurred, the words in this book are meant to provoke, inspire, rattle, and soothe the soul of recovery. As with anyone's personal therapeutic experience, sometimes it is an off-hand comment and sometimes an incredibly profound interpretation or insight that changes us, and what matters is that it does. What is clear is that remaining stagnant will leave one exactly where one is, the same place. May this book help with healing and moving forward, even if that may look like taking two steps back from time to time.

Stephanie Yoder, PsyD

Stephanie Yoder, Psy.D., a Licensed Psychologist, is currently the Chief Operating Officer for Malvern Treatment Centers, Ford Road in Philadelphia. Previously, she worked at Brooke Glen Behavioral Hospital for 20 years, where she served as Director of Clinical Services. Dr. Yoder received her doctorate in clinical psychology from Widener University, with concentrations in cognitive-behavioral therapy, industrial-organizational psychology, and psychological assessment. She received her undergraduate degree in psychology from the Pennsylvania State University, where she worked as a research assistant in the personality lab.

Dr. Yoder is passionate about providing empirically based treatment with an emphasis on providing compassionate, trauma-informed care. She particularly enjoys mentoring and educating staff and students, as well as developing programming for underserved clinical populations. She has supervised over 100 students pursuing advanced degrees in clinical psychology. Through that work, she received the Outstanding Supervisor Award from Widener University in 2011 and served as adjunct faculty at Widener University and Philadelphia College of Osteopathic Medicine. Dr. Yoder's clinical interests include personality assessment (particularly including the Rorschach), trauma work, and empirically based treatments for serious mental illness.

INTRODUCTION

Welcome.

Whether you're holding this book because you're struggling with addiction, supporting someone who is, working in the field of mental health, or simply curious about the recovery journey, I'm grateful you're here.

The Power of Recovery is not just a collection of stories. It's a chorus of voices—raw, real, and profoundly human—sharing what it means to fall apart, rebuild, and keep going. In these pages, you will meet people from all walks of life who have battled addiction, mental illness, trauma, and loss. Their stories are not neat. They're not sanitized. But they are powerful.

This book is divided into two sections. The first features deeply personal narratives of addiction and recovery. These are stories of rock bottom and redemption, of resilience forged in pain, and of the quiet miracles that happen when someone chooses life—again and again. The second section offers a person-centered guide for individuals at various stages of the recovery journey: those who are struggling, those actively working on their recovery, and those who love someone who is. This section also includes tools, resources, and reflections meant to encourage and support healing.

One of the most insidious parts of addiction is the shame that surrounds it. Shame isolates. It convinces us that we are alone. These stories challenge that belief. They remind us that recovery is possible, that healing is not linear, and that connection is essential. If you take away one thing from this book, let it be this: You are not alone.

You'll notice that some contributors use humor, some use hard-earned wisdom, and others offer vulnerable glimpses into the darkest moments of their lives. Each voice is different, but the underlying message is the same: recovery is not only possible, it's powerful.

We also know that recovery doesn't end after detox or treatment. Recovery is an ongoing process that includes discovering purpose, reconnecting with community, and learning to live with compassion—for yourself and others. It's about building a life that's not only free from substances but also full of meaning.

As someone who is in long-term recovery myself, I can tell you that the road isn't always easy, but it's worth every step. I hope that this book becomes a companion to you or someone you care about. Something you can return to when you need a reminder that people do change, healing happens, and there is strength in vulnerability.

Thank you to every person who bravely shared their story. And thank you, the reader, for being part of this journey. Whether you're here for understanding, support, or inspiration, I hope this book serves as a reminder of the extraordinary power of recovery—and of the incredible strength that already lives within you.

With gratitude and hope,
Patrick McElwaine, PsyD
Dr. Mac

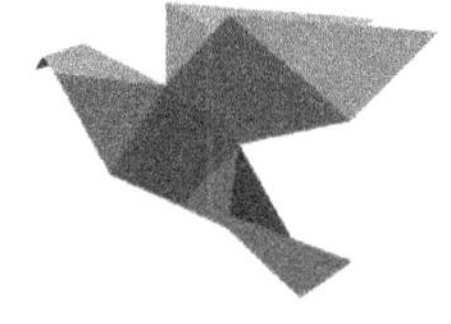

CHAPTER 1

Thank You Recovery, You Saved My Life!
Patrick McElwaine, PsyD

On my ninth birthday, we went to the Pocono Mountains instead of the usual Jersey Shore. The excitement of being somewhere new, especially on my birthday, was thrilling. Surrounded by pine trees, cool mountain air, and my family, everything felt amazing. The week was full of swimming, basketball with my dad, adventures with my siblings, and fun with new friends.

I grew up in a row home in Northeast Philadelphia, Pennsylvania. My father was a Philadelphia fireman, and my mother was a stay-at-home mom. I am the oldest of three children. My sister, Melissa, is two years younger than I am, and my brother, Steven, is five years younger. All in all, we had a happy childhood. My parents were loving, caring, and devoted to us. For the first nine years of my life, everything felt simple and fun; life without a care in the world. That summer trip to the mountains felt like just another adventure, an extension of the safe, happy life we had always known. I didn't realize those days of simplicity and security were coming to an end.

Our last day of vacation was on July 17th. That evening, my dad asked if I wanted to take a walk with him as I played outside with my brother, sister, and new friends that we had met. I told my dad I wanted to keep playing with my friends, not knowing it would be the last time I would speak with him.

The next morning, I woke up expecting to get ready for the ride home, but something felt off. My dad wasn't in the room. I remember glancing around, feeling a pit in my stomach. Before I could process it, the resort manager came in and told us something had happened to my father, essentially letting us know that he had passed away. My brother and sister quickly left the room to go to my mom, but I froze, staring out the window as tears slid down my cheeks and I remembered the sun hitting me in the face. I would eventually get out of bed, and I always remember the feeling of opening the door, seeing lots of people in this small cabin, and my mom coming to me and hugging me. I remember her crying, and everything seemed to be in slow motion. This day would change the world I live in and my life forever!

What we believe happened to my dad was that during his walk, he stopped by the cabin of a couple we had befriended that week to visit and say goodbye. He had a few beers with them, which emboldened him to go down the slide headfirst, something he had talked about doing after watching the kids do it all week but had been too embarrassed to do it in front of everyone. He had to pass the pool to get back to our cabin. So, we presume, my dad finally worked up the courage to go down the resort's curvy pool slide since no one was around. On the evening of July 17th, he folded his clothes next to a chair, along with a bag containing two cans of Budweiser. The police reported that someone in one of the cabins near the pool heard splashing and coughing around 11 p.m., but did not check it out. Their interview with the police was also cut short because they were too emotional to continue. The official cause of death was drowning.

At that moment, my childhood came to an end. My mom, who had once been a stay-at-home parent with my dad as the provider, was suddenly a single mother of three. She had to carry her grief while comforting ours, making sure we were cared for emotionally and mentally. Holidays in the beginning were brutal. That first Christmas, the emptiness of my father's absence sat heavier than the gifts under the tree. Yet my mom, though broken in ways I couldn't fully understand, did everything she could to shield us. She showed us resilience not through speeches but through action: keeping routines, cooking meals, sitting with us in our sadness, and always being there for us through everything. She put her children's needs before her own and showed us that, although we were hurting, we were loved. She reminded us that even in loss, we still had one another.

During my pre-teen years, I would struggle with the grief of losing my dad, being bullied, and having low self-esteem and confidence. At first, I played the role of the "good kid," even reporting to my mom when friends drank. I would come home from being out with friends and tell my mom everything everyone was doing and how I didn't participate in the partying and drinking beer. That stopped at fourteen, when I picked up my first drink. I remember the first time drinking a beer and hating it; it tasted disgusting to me. I also knew that alcohol played a role in my dad's death, so that was extra motivation not to drink. I would tell a friend walking home that day that I am never drinking again; it was horrible. That weekend, I would be offered another drink, and I would get drunk for the first time, and I knew from that night on that alcohol would be a significant part of my life. I felt the pain disappear. For the first time in years, I felt like I belonged. Alcohol gave me a mask to wear. Behind it, I could be confident, bold, even invincible. I could finally talk confidently to girls, and to my surprise, they would talk back and even like me. I could stick up for myself and others who were getting picked on. I got into my first fight and found out I could fight. I could actually fight back pretty well, and bullying came to an end. I felt that alcohol gave me all these gifts!

Alcohol became my escape hatch: from my father's death, from bullying at school, from a voice inside me that whispered I wasn't good enough. Parties, sneaking drinks with friends, near misses behind the wheel of a car; it all blurred into a reckless rhythm. At twenty, my doctor told me my liver was already showing damage. Before the discussion with my doctor, I was drinking a lot; it became a big part of my life. I remember the conversation with my doctor about my liver very clearly. He brought me into the office and asked me about my drinking. I told him I didn't drink that much, occasionally on the weekend, but that's about it. He would slam his clipboard on the desk and say, "Do you think this is a joke? Your drinking is showing problems with your liver (a fatty liver), and if you continue drinking, you will die from this." I remember being shocked by this. I had a great relationship with my doctor, talking about Penn State football, the Eagles, family stuff, and now I was getting yelled at about my drinking. He cared so much about me; he was fearful of what drinking was doing to me, especially after I lied to him about it. I stopped drinking for six months and focused on working out. I was in great physical, mental, and emotional shape. I did this all by myself! Someone who is an alcoholic couldn't do this by themselves, couldn't stop on their own for six months, right?

But when a vacation to the Jersey Shore came around, I would go out and buy a six-pack of beer before we decided on playing a board game together. The look of disappointment in my family's eyes was evident. I said that I was fine. That I hadn't had any alcohol in six months, which should have told them I didn't have a problem. I would wind up drinking the six-pack, going out that night, and having another blackout drunk night.

I wish I could say my wake-up call came early. Instead, addiction dug its claws deeper. I met Elyse, who would become my wife, while working at a residential treatment facility. I thought my charm won her over, but the truth is my drinking nearly drove her away. To keep her, I went to AA and therapy. My sobriety date was June 23, 2005, but it was a hollow milestone. I wasn't doing it for me; I was doing it to hang onto a relationship.

Relapses followed. I would be a chronic relapser from 2005 to 2009, sometimes being able to put together a few months, and sometimes not being able to get a day. The trust in my family and with Elyse was gone. Alcohol was winning this battle, and I just couldn't manage it at all; it was destroying my life. Then, a "friend" handed me some painkillers, benzodiazepines, and opiates, promising they were easier to conceal. What started as a cover quickly became my prison. A day in active addiction looked like this: wake up groggy, promise myself today would be different, use before breakfast, lie to my wife, hide bottles or pills, show up to work half-present, then plan my next drink or pill before I'd even finished the first. I hated myself for it. Yet I couldn't stop. I was a chronic relapser, stringing together days at best. Each failure chipped away at my hope until I honestly believed recovery wasn't possible for me.

By February 2009, the exhaustion of living two lives—public therapist, private addict—was killing me. I would have had a few significant events that could have ended more tragically than they did. On February 12, 2009, I walked back into a twelve-step meeting. Fear gripped me, but so did desperation. I knew if I kept going, I'd lose everything: my marriage, my career, even my life. That desperation finally outweighed my fear. A week later, sitting in a psychiatrist's office, I shared with him my life story; I knew how to share it; I had done this many times before. At the end, I asked him the question that haunted me: "Why does this keep happening to me?" His answer was blunt: "Because you're an alcoholic and a drug addict." He said it eight times in one session. I left, furious. As a therapist, I thought he had broken every rule about empathy and rapport. I was a therapist. I know that before you say these types of things to a client, you should have a good therapeutic relationship, there should be trust and rapport, but what he did was point a finger at me eight different times and call me an addict and an alcoholic. I wanted to hit him!

I called Elyse, ranting as I drove home from the session on Interstate 95. She listened quietly and then said, "Pat, you might want to take a closer look at why you're so angry about what he said." I handled it very maturely. I cursed her out and threw the phone on the floor. I hit the gas, and I was angry! Then her words hit me. The truth was, I wasn't mad at being judged; I was mad at myself for not wanting to accept who I was. I hated the stigma of being "an addict," "an alcoholic," or someone who is in recovery. I wanted people to see me as Pat, the funny guy, the nice guy, the Eagles fan, the good therapist, and a good person. Admitting the label felt like admitting I was broken. But denying it was destroying me.

That suffocating realization cracked something open. I went back to the psychiatrist, and he was surprised I came back. I let him know about my discussion with my wife and how I felt about the previous session. He told me he said it because I needed to hear it. For the first time, I stopped running. I accepted the truth: yes, I am an alcoholic and an addict. And strangely, acceptance didn't crush me; it freed me.

Recovery hasn't been easy. Early on, the cravings were unbearable. I sat in meetings with my hands shaking, my mind screaming for a drink and a drug. There were days I drove past a liquor store and had to pull over just to breathe. I had setbacks, moments of doubt, and times when I questioned whether I was strong enough or if I could do this. But there were also moments of grace, the first sober holiday, laughing with my family and actually remembering it; the first time Elyse told me she trusted me again; the birth of our daughters, Morgan and Eva, moments for which I was fully present.

Recovery gave me more than sobriety; it gave me back my life. I returned to school, earned my doctorate, worked in various therapeutic settings, and then in academia. I found purpose in helping others. I built a family life filled with laughter, love, and with my beloved pets, Vinnie, who sadly passed away in October of 2021, and currently, Charlie.

I've also found joy in simple passions. Cheering for the Eagles, remembering every play, hugging my daughters before bedtime, walking into a classroom, and watching students discover their own potential. These highs wouldn't mean as much if I hadn't endured the lows.

I still attend meetings and therapy—not because I'm broken, but because I want to stay well. When I first started out in recovery, I hated meetings, hated therapy, and thought short and long-term recovery were impossible for me. Now, I love my sessions and twelve-step meetings; I am proud of the person I am today, and I know that without this support, I wouldn't be where I am right now. Recovery has taught me that life doesn't get easier, but I've grown stronger to meet it. I can enjoy my passions again, like cheering for my Eagles, and yes, I remember the games now. I've watched them win two Super Bowls in sobriety, and although I still can't get my two daughters to love football and the Eagles (a parenting fail in my opinion). I feel immense gratitude and love in my life.

To anyone reading this who feels hopeless, here's my advice:

Don't wait for the "right time." There isn't one. Start where you are, even if it's messy.

You are not your addiction. You are more than your worst day, more than your relapses.

Lean on others. Recovery is a team sport; you can't do it alone.

Celebrate small wins. A single day sober is a victory. Collect enough of those, and they change your life.

I once believed I wouldn't make it. Today, I live a life I never thought possible. Recovery won't give you your old life back: it will give you a new one, richer and fuller than you imagine. I am no longer ashamed of my journey. I am strong. I am resilient. I am empowered. And I am living proof that recovery saves lives. Thank you for allowing me to share my story with you! I hope it helps!

Patrick McElwaine, PsyD

Dr. Patrick McElwaine (Dr. Mac) is a Licensed Clinical Psychologist, Licensed Professional Counselor (LPC), a Beck Institute Certified Cognitive Behavior Therapy (CBT) clinician and Certified EMDR Clinician (EMDR-C), integrating evidence-based approaches in his work with trauma, mental health, and substance use. He serves as Associate Professor and Program Director of the Graduate Counseling Psychology Program at Moravian University. He is also a faculty member at the Beck Institute. In addition, Dr. McElwaine is the founder of Dr. Mac and Associates, a private practice committed to supporting mental health and recovery.

Dr. McElwaine is a columnist for *Psychology Today*, where he writes about addiction, recovery, resilience, and mental health. He has over 29 years of clinical experience in a wide range of settings, including community mental health, primary care, private practice, wrap-around services, residential treatment facilities, inpatient hospitals, and academia. Through his work at the Beck Institute, Dr. McElwaine provides supervision, consultation, and facilitates workshops focused on Cognitive Behavior Therapy (CBT) for substance use, depression, anxiety, suicide prevention, and trauma. He is a member of several professional psychology organizations and serves on the Montgomery

County Drug and Alcohol Advisory Council and on the Board of Trustees for the Bucks County chapter of the National Alliance on Mental Illness (NAMI).

Dr. McElwaine is a passionate speaker and educator, having presented at national and regional conferences including NAMI, the Pennsylvania Psychological Association (PPA), Mindscape Conference, the Lilly Conference, and others. His presentations focus on mental health, addiction, stigma reduction, and innovative approaches to teaching and therapy.

He is also in long-term recovery from alcohol and drug addiction, with 17 years of sustained recovery. Dr. McElwaine believes deeply in the connection between substance use disorders and mental health issues such as anxiety, depression, trauma, and grief. He is a strong advocate for those affected by mental illness and addiction, often stating, *"Those in recovery or living with mental health conditions are resilient, strong, and empowered."*

Outside of his professional life, Dr. McElwaine enjoys spending time with his wife, two daughters, and their dog. He is an avid sports fan and a diehard Philadelphia Eagles fan.

https://www.drmactherapy.com/

https://beckinstitute.org/about/our-team/faculty/patrick-mcelwaine-psyd/

https://www.linkedin.com/in/patrick-mcelwaine-4b635316/

CHAPTER 2

I L-O-V-E, LOVE Drugs
(But That's Not the Whole Story)
Will Herman, LMSW

Addiction doesn't come crashing into your life all at once; it creeps in, disguising itself as relief, connection, or even love. For me, it began with a restless mind and a chaotic home. I latched onto anything that promised an escape.

Let's get one thing straight: I L-O-V-E, *LOVE* drugs. I always have, and I probably always will. But the feeling was never mutual—drugs didn't love me back, and they definitely didn't love my life. What began as a harmless experiment quickly unraveled into years of dependence, loss, and upheaval. But through the pain came resilience, recovery, and a life rebuilt from the ground up.

I took my first hit of cannabis in a moment of hopelessness and curiosity, inviting drugs into my life at twelve years old. Yeah, I was an early bloomer like that. Looking back, my early fascination with drugs wasn't random; it was rooted in anxiety and a desperate need for comfort. Growing up with a father who has narcissistic personality disorder, and an emotionally unavailable mother exposed me to trauma in spades. Trauma, combined with a lack of emotional support, created a perfect storm.

On top of that, I have (and have always had) an overactive and sensitive nervous system, which contributes to a constant undercurrent of anxiety in my life. I never felt comfortable in my own skin as a child. I remember having anxiety so bad that I would literally want to jump out of my skin because it felt like it didn't fit and was on fire. The best example of this is when my parents would argue. The feeling of 9.9/10 anxiety coupled with the fear of abandonment, made my young mind feel out of control. I also never learned how to regulate my emotions, and I never had a chance to see how it was done, so I couldn't. To be honest, I'm still not really good at that one, but I'm working on it.

I can see now that I had some very serious mental health issues going on. Little did I know that my childhood anxiety was a symptom of deeper psychological concerns that would later shape my relationship with drugs. In fifth grade, the well-meaning but comically misinformed cops from the D.A.R.E. program lectured our class, telling us how awesome the effects of drugs could be. That's what I heard, anyway. I was especially interested in the ones known as "depressants," which slowed down the nervous system. Mmmmmm, a slowed-down nervous system. Such a simple yet tantalizing idea. Could this be the answer I was looking for?

That curiosity sparked my desire to experiment with mind-altering substances. One fateful day after school, I went to a friend's house with the intention of smoking cannabis. I was euphoric at just the thought of what being "high" might be like; the D.A.R.E. officer made it sound amazing. Upon my first inhale of cannabis at twelve years old, its smoke seemed to release me from the excruciatingly tight grip my feverish nervous system had imposed on me since birth. Smoking out of a homemade bong in my friend's house made my psyche, my very soul, sigh a deep sigh of relief. I didn't have all those torturous feelings weighing on my chest, and my skin seemed to fit much more naturally.

From that moment on, all I wanted was to be high. Normal life would no longer cut it. Knowing there was relief and a "better" way to live, I finally felt like I could breathe and be myself. I didn't care what my parents said or did when I was high, so naturally, I chased that feeling.

My priorities quickly shifted from school and fun to finding ways to leave my house to get high. Many of my early friendships were destroyed because I was so absorbed in my new hobby that I failed to see how I was neglecting and mistreating everyone around me. I cared, but not enough to stop using. Sitting in an assembly one afternoon, I listened to the speaker discuss the progression of his drug use. He said, "I started off smoking weed with my friends after school. I never thought I'd do heroin." I turned to my friend and remarked, "Getting stoned is enough for me. I don't understand why anyone would do anything other than weed."

That mentality didn't last long.

As my focus edged even further from my education and wholesome hobbies, I started gravitating toward people who shared my true passion: getting high. I had a friend whose sister sold weed, and their mother had prescriptions for opioids and other narcotics. He liked to share. That relationship led me to neglect my true friends, and I suffered greatly for it. To fill the void, I surrounded myself with a new crowd—not so much friends as "running mates," who valued me less as a person and more as a convenient way to get high.

Around this time, smoking cannabis evolved from a fun thing I did to quiet my nervous system to more of a chore. Constantly craving the high while knowing my real friends disapproved of the "new me" was soul-crushing, but it only pushed me to keep going. My life was slipping away from me. My high school memories are forever tainted by the decisions I made to put my relationship with drugs first.

I started college with almost no friends, mainly because of my own actions, seeking a fresh start. When I got there, I was a mess. But I found a new friend group and, most importantly, drugs. While I never put myself in immediate mortal danger, I definitely got into situations that were way less than (this is the level of detail I am comfortable with) safe. After nearly three and a half years, my drug use finally caught up with me. There was only so much schooling I could do while keeping up with my usage. I could not go to class full-time and continue to use. Due to the stress of it all, I had a severe emotional breakdown that landed me in the hospital. I could not stop crying and felt like I wanted to die. I was discharged about twenty-four hours after with antipsychotics and sent on my way. A few weeks later, things did not improve. I left school and moved back home. At the time, I couldn't imagine anything worse.

I went from having my freedom to being back under the thumb of my emotionally abusive parents. The thought of living with these people again terrified me. After taking some time to recover from my physical illness, I started working at my father's business. Working for my father caused extreme depression because all he would do was yell at me and refuse to show me complex things more than once. I naturally chose drugs to help me feel better. That's when I was introduced to a new drug: dope (heroin). I had used opioids and opiates in the past, but, in my mind, I'd never crossed the line into the "hard stuff." If cannabis took the edge off the pain, dope obliterated it. Unfortunately, dope's honeymoon phase doesn't last very long. Before I knew it, I had a problem.

You know that line you have in your head, the one that marks how far you're willing to take something? Initially, my line was not using any drugs besides cannabis. That changed within two years when I tried ketamine, mushrooms, and prescription pills. After that, I didn't really care about trying new drugs as long as I wasn't using heroin. I figured, as long as I wasn't using heroin, I was still doing okay. But that line shifted, too, until I found myself crossing it.

At first, I would just sniff it. At least I wasn't *injecting* it. Then, someone pointed out that I could use less if I injected it. At least I wasn't *smoking crack*. Being told it was cheaper was all it took, and that was that. Anything that will save a drug user money is the best thing ever, so naturally, I just did it. This went on for about six months until I lost my job at my family's business. By that point, I barely felt human. I wasn't bathing, brushing my teeth, or changing my clothes regularly.

Now, I finally understood true desperation. I knew what it was like to feel complete alienation and isolation. I felt the crushing weight of compounded shame, guilt, and self-hatred. The problems I'd originally been escaping seemed like a vacation compared to the absolute horror and despair of opioid addiction. It felt like a slow death. My heart, my very spirit, was hollow and dead. How did this happen? How did I go from smoking weed with friends to nearly losing everything to dope?

The answer was that the line in the sand I'd drawn kept moving. Hitting rock bottom was inevitable, and it wasn't long before I found myself in a place I never imagined I'd end up in: rehab. Well, if you insist on being accurate, first two weeks in the psych unit—then rehab.

The psych unit didn't exactly live up to its name. Located in a hospital basement, this particular facility may have had the "unit" locked down, but the "psych" aspect was severely lacking. It was unlike anything I'd ever experienced. No glasses, no shoelaces, no belt. I needed that stuff! I was going through withdrawal, stuck in a dungeon with zero comforts. Man, that was a rude awakening. After seeing daily takedowns, forced medication, and five-point holds on patients, I was more than ready to try rehab.

I knew I wanted to feel better, and everyone kept telling me this was the way. Somewhere inside, I knew they were right. For the first time, I recognized that I wasn't just trying to escape the world around me; I was trying to escape my own trauma and self-loathing, the feelings that I'm not good enough and that my past will always define me. In the quiet moments, amidst the chaos, I realized that recovery wasn't just a path others were recommending; it was something I needed to reclaim my sense of self.

At this point, I witnessed another new and unsettling sight: my father crying. He had just learned I was using heroin. Let me set the scene for you. I'm in this hellhole, in withdrawal and feeling as low as a human being can. In walks my parents. I can feel how mad and disgusted they are at me. I can smell their disappointment. Then my father speaks, "It had to be heroin?" He begins to cry and leaves the room. This hit me very hard because, at the time, I actually cared about his opinion. My parents, after attending some Nar-Anon meetings, presented me with an ultimatum: if I relapsed, I would be out of the family and out of the house. They wouldn't enable me. That reality shook me. I wanted to get better because I sincerely wanted to be the "good son" back then, and I knew they meant what they said.

When I arrived at the next facility—a legit treatment center, not a hospital basement—I finally received actual treatment. I started a medication regimen while learning about coping skills and the science behind mental health and addiction. Surprisingly, I found these topics genuinely interesting, more than most other things I'd studied before. But the most meaningful part of my stay was the family session, during which my therapist met with my parents and me to discuss my next steps.

During this session, I was advised to attend ninety meetings of Alcoholics Anonymous in ninety days and that I might be a good fit to become a CASAC: A Credentialed Alcoholism and Substance Abuse

Counselor. I'd never heard of this before, but I was definitely intrigued. Sitting across from my parents, I was reminded by their serious demeanor of the consequences I'd face for relapsing, namely being homeless, which gave me the motivation I needed to see this through. But more importantly, I realized I wanted to get better *not* for them, but for the version of myself I had almost forgotten (or perhaps never given myself the chance to become)—a person who could heal and thrive beyond the confines of addiction and mental health issues.

After leaving rehab, I completed my "90 in 90" meetings and attended clinic-based services. As luck would have it, those clinic services were terrible. Back in 2008, substance abuse treatment was still heavily punitive and centered on the twelve-step model. Many clinics also borrowed from the Therapeutic Community approach, by which a person is "broken down" before they are "built back up."

This type of treatment did not work for me. I didn't need to be broken down; I was already there—worn down by my own actions and circumstances. What I needed was warmth and understanding, not to relive my childhood trauma. During this time, I also received a lot of professional advice that, while well-intended, was questionable at best. Mantras like "Just don't use," "Go to meetings and you'll be fine," and "Let go and let God" may have worked for others, but they fell flat for me. Generic slogans wouldn't heal me; I needed help that was tailored to my unique blend of biology and trauma.

While the standard treatment approaches fell short, one person helped me stay afloat. At this point, I connected with an outside therapist who skillfully guided me through this challenging period. Early on, she confronted my mother, firmly telling her to back off and let me figure things out for myself, something I desperately needed to have a real chance of healing.

She also introduced me to the concept of personifying mental illness, referring to my addiction as "the monster that lives inside." Unlike the Therapeutic Community approach, this perspective was constructive; it reduced the self-loathing I felt for letting things get so far out of control. My therapist's willingness to meet me where I was, coupled with my growing belief in a better future, became the spark that reignited my drive to fight for recovery.

Things were finally looking up. Although I was bouncing from one crappy job to another, there was light at the end of the tunnel. After being laid off from a particularly soul-crushing position, I entered a program through unemployment that paid me while I went back to school. Through this program, I earned a Bachelor of Science in Community and Human Services with a concentration in Substance Abuse Services, which ultimately led to me receiving a CASAC-Trainee certificate.

In my last semester of undergrad, after fighting tooth and nail, I eventually secured an internship placement at the very facility where I had been a patient only four years earlier. Stepping into the day room for the first time, now with a badge and keys to the unit, was a very proud moment. Everything was finally coming full circle. I threw myself into that internship with the passion of a man on fire. I was genuinely excited to be there every day, feeling that this was the biggest accomplishment of my life.

My newfound happiness and enthusiasm didn't go unnoticed by my coworkers and supervisors, who told me they'd "see what they could do for me" when I finished the internship. Well, I got the job and worked there for two years, a period of significant personal and professional growth. During this time, I married the love of my life, further grounding me in a sense of stability and purpose. It was also then that I realized a bachelor's degree would only take me so far in the mental health field, prompting me to return to school and earn a Master of Social Work degree—my second greatest accomplishment.

Since earning my degree and becoming a licensed social worker, I've worked in public mental health clinics, a hospital, and on a 35-foot RV providing in-community harm reduction services. Currently, I work in private practice, specializing in narcissistic abuse, adverse childhood events, and sex therapy. I've truly found my place in the field, and I'm happier with my career than I ever imagined I could be.

My sobriety has afforded me a livelihood and a life far richer than I could have dreamed of when I was using. I've been married to my love for eleven years, and we have two beautiful boys together. It's this profound sense of gratitude that inspires me to share what I've learned, hoping to give back to others on their journey. My own experience and the wisdom of those who came before me have taught me invaluable lessons. These are not absolute truths—just the way I see things.

The most important thing *not* to do to someone in recovery is to judge them. The person is likely already judging themselves harshly, so adding fuel to the fire only makes it harder for them to maintain their drive. Even well-intentioned "tough love" doesn't work for those struggling with addiction. Telling someone they're trash usually isn't compelling motivation. Instead, try being supportive.

To be clear, "supportive" isn't interchangeable with "enabling." Being supportive means that when this person asks for help (within reason), you help them. It does not mean bailing out your adult child after they've spent their rent money on drugs. If you truly want someone to get better and they're sincerely trying their best, you can express your feelings without passing judgment. For example, you might say, "It upsets me that you're using," instead of, "You're a piece of shit for using." Cruelty doesn't encourage most people to stay clean.

Another critical lesson I've learned along this journey is that recovery doesn't just mean abstinence. It's also about adopting compassionate policies that support safer use. This brings us to harm reduction, a simple but powerful concept: people are going to use drugs anyway, so let's minimize the risks to them and their communities. Methadone, for example, is an opioid that works like heroin but lasts much longer. Dispensed at licensed clinics, it provides steady effects, helping users maintain employment and avoid criminal activity to support their use.

I first discovered harm reduction while seeking effective yet underutilized ways to help others. At the time, real-world examples were rare, but the literature and models such as Canada's and Switzerland's safe injection sites showed promise. I was excited to find innovative approaches for challenging cases. Over the years, I've seen Suboxone, an opioid that satisfies the brain's cravings with few other noticeable effects, help nearly one hundred people regain control of their lives.

One client, a man who'd been injecting morphine since age nine, with no desire to stop, was shocked and terrified when his urine toxicology revealed he was only using fentanyl, not heroin—a sight I'll never forget. The day he agreed to try Suboxone, his outlook began to shift. He completed treatment, satisfied probation, and stayed clean. Harm reduction offers a lifeline for those who are not ready or able to pursue abstinence. Its benefits are undeniable—not just for the individual, but for society as a whole.

Perhaps the most crucial part of an individual's recovery is the reason this chapter is called "I L-O-V-E, *LOVE* drugs." It's true—I love drugs. Yet, I've had to come to terms with the fact that I cannot use drugs and have a happy and functional life. Getting here took a long time, but I'm at peace with it now. This is called acceptance. Acceptance, for me, doesn't mean denying that recovery is a loss in some way. I've mourned that loss in different ways over time, but it has led to seventeen years (3/14/08) and counting of sobriety from heroin.

I don't resent my past; I understand it. Loving drugs may have been part of my story, but learning to L-O-V-E, *LOVE* life (without drugs) became the ultimate challenge and reward. Every day, I choose this path, grateful for the chance to share my experience and help others rewrite their own stories. Recovery isn't just a destination; it's a journey that has taught me the value of acceptance, the strength in vulnerability, and the importance of meeting people where they are. I hope this trip through my life inspires more compassion, understanding, and hope for anyone who might be struggling.

Will Herman, LMSW

Will Herman, Licensed Master Social Worker, has been dedicated to the field of mental health since 2011. He holds a Bachelor of Science in Community and Human Services with a focus on Substance Abuse Services from Empire State College and earned his Master of Social Work from Stony Brook University.

Will is known for his person-centered, nonjudgmental approach, fostering a supportive environment where clients feel empowered to pursue their well-being. He believes individuals are the experts of their own lives and collaborates with clients to respect their unique experiences. Will's work focuses on helping clients achieve their goals by utilizing their strengths and building tools for personal growth and lasting change.

Outside of work, Will is married and the proud father of two boys. He enjoys spending time with his family, playing video games, and participating in Dungeons & Dragons.

"Be the change that you wish to see in the world." –Mahatma Gandhi

Email: wherman1@gmail.com

CHAPTER 3

Thank God for Drugs and Alcohol: Finding Purpose in the Pain
Jessica Osborn, MS, CAADC, CRS, CCTP

Thank God for Drugs and Alcohol. That may seem like a strange thing to say in a story about recovery, but stay with me. For much of my life, darkness and pain defined my story—or rather, a search for an escape from that darkness and pain. I clung tightly to anything that offered a reprieve, however temporary. Drugs and alcohol promised that reprieve, and for a while, they delivered. But ultimately, addiction wasn't the escape I needed it to be. It was a symptom of the deeper wounds I carried, the ones I didn't know how to heal. It wasn't until I reached rock bottom that I began to understand: the pain I tried so desperately to avoid was pointing me toward my purpose.

Trauma has been a persistent thread throughout my life. I was molested at four, sexually assaulted at sixteen, and viciously raped and beaten as a young adult in the military. For over fifteen years, I held onto that secret alone. People did not openly discuss sexual assault in the military in the early 2000s. As a staff sergeant, I felt I couldn't tell anyone what happened to me because I was sure they'd see me as weak or damaged, and frankly, that wasn't something I could accept. Even with all of that, I loved the military. Despite everything I endured, the experience gave me what I needed when I needed it most: structure.

Unfortunately, my military career—and with it, my sense of structure—was cut short. I was medically retired from the Air Force in January 2009, after being diagnosed with endometriosis, which left me in chronic pain. I underwent multiple surgeries to try to manage the condition, but nothing was successful. Thankfully, I had already had my three children before eventually needing a full hysterectomy, unaware that the pain could persist even after the surgery. Pain management became the only avenue left to pursue. At the peak of my treatment, I was prescribed 120 Percocet pills per month, forty milligrams of methadone per day, and eight tablets of fentanyl per month.

As if that wasn't enough, I was also taking Ambien for insomnia, a lasting effect of the trauma from the sexual assault. On top of that, I had also been diagnosed with major depressive disorder, generalized anxiety disorder, post-traumatic stress disorder, and obsessive-compulsive disorder. I was on a vast array of medications to attempt to control both my mental and physical health, but none of these pills could supplement what I was really lacking: my identity. Without the military, I didn't know who I was anymore. That's when I let drugs and alcohol define me instead.

For seven years this continued, my depression getting worse and worse. Despite faithfully attending my psychiatrist and therapy appointments, I could find no peace beyond sleeping my life away. Every morning, I'd wake up counting the hours until I could take another pill to escape into sleep again. My then husband would ask me, "What do you have to be so miserable about?" And the truth was, I didn't know. I couldn't explain what I was feeling or what I was going through. Being sad or miserable wasn't an act; inside, I was drowning. This just added to the thoughts in my head that there was something inherently wrong with me. If my own husband, who knew everything about me, thought I should be okay, then maybe I was dramatic, perhaps it was a me issue.

I felt defined by everything that I wasn't. Outside of the military, I never felt comfortable in my own skin. I'm not your typical "girly girl"—I love the Eagles, I enjoy watching MMA, and I have no interest in scrapbooking. I didn't feel like the type of mom my kids deserved. I didn't carry wet wipes or snacks; in fact, I usually didn't even carry a purse. Every small omission felt like proof that I wasn't enough. I felt that no matter how hard I tried, I didn't fit in and never would. Eventually, the pain of being me became too great, and I could see only one way out.

On Wednesday, June 1, 2016, I took my kids out on the slip-and-slide. We ate all their favorite foods because I knew, with absolute certainty, that the next day I was going to kill myself. And that's exactly what I tried to do. The following Thursday, I took every pill in my medicine cabinet, expecting to drift off peacefully, the way it looks in the movies. That was not my experience. Instead, my body became paralyzed, and I started choking on my own vomit. I urinated and defecated on myself until eventually I lost consciousness.

The only reason I am alive today is because my daughter was sent home from school with a stomachache. She spent the afternoon with her dad, playing a game where they would spit straw wrappers at each other. When she went to look for the trash can, she found it upstairs because Mommy was "sick again." And that's when she found me, essentially dead on the bed. Her dad rushed upstairs and performed CPR until the paramedics arrived. Naturally, this was the day before my daughter's birthday, because that's the type of mom I was in my active addiction: selfish. I wasn't concerned that her birthday would be eternally tethered to that horrific scene—a memory she'd carry whether I lived or died.

When I woke up, I wasn't relieved that I didn't die; I was upset, thinking, *I can't even kill myself right.* Of course, I ended up in a psych ward for a few days, but I managed to convince the "trained professionals" that I was only using substances to get up the nerve to kill myself. There were no questions asked about me about how long I was using, what I was using, or what I was trying to escape from. The therapists just saw that I had attempted suicide and assumed that I was only taking the pills to help in that endeavor. So, when I was discharged, nothing changed. I left with the same pain, the same emptiness, and the same destructive habits that had brought me there in the first place. Actually, one thing was different: now, I felt even more hopeless. My failure at dying was proof I couldn't escape my life or myself.

Six months later, I was a pharmacy technician, and it had become apparent that I would not be able to continue in that job, for obvious reasons. I was out of money and out of a job, so I found myself detoxing cold turkey from a sizable number of opiates. On the third day, my brain snapped. I was told that I grabbed a knife, missing my youngest son's head by inches, and threatened to kill myself again because of my physical and emotional pain.

Consistent with the self-centered patterns I had fallen into then, this was also the day before my oldest son's birthday. At this point, my family had finally reached its breaking point. They gave me an ultimatum that I know was the most difficult thing they had ever had to say to me: *go to treatment or be homeless.* Feeling backed into a corner, I decided to go.

Although I went to treatment reluctantly, it was there that I encountered a therapist who would shift my perspective, helping me to see a glimmer of hope in a life I had all but given up on. The therapist, who I met during my time in the psych ward, identified as being in recovery. He asked me to share my story, which, of course, was nothing but pain and sadness. But this is where my walls started to crack, just a little; it was the first time that I had allowed someone into the darkness consuming my life. I finally let myself cry—not just a tear or two, but real, gut-wrenching sobs.

This therapist was the first person who believed in me, even before I believed in myself. He often spoke about resilience, empowerment, and strength. "That's what recovery is, and that's what you are," he'd say. He couldn't have known how much I needed to hear those words. He was the first person I'd met who was truly living in recovery, and seeing him gave me hope that things could actually get better. He didn't look miserable or take himself too seriously; he seemed genuinely happy—something I was craving. For the first time, I saw a glimpse of what a sober, fulfilling life could look like, and I decided to give this recovery thing a try. But I knew it wouldn't be easy.

While in rehab, I listened to speakers from the various twelve-step programs. Many shared one piece of advice: go to a recovery house. I decided immediately that once I was discharged, I'd find one and go. Not one person in my life supported this. I was a wife and mom to three children; I was supposed to go back to my family. But I knew I couldn't do that. If I did what everyone else wanted, I would die, most likely by my own hand. It wasn't my family's fault; I just couldn't get better in Levittown. I knew a change of scenery was a gamble, but it was one I had to take.

That's when I moved to York, Pennsylvania. I knew I needed a fresh start, and York was close enough (within driving distance) that I could still visit my kids, but far enough away to avoid temptations from my previous life. Surviving the move without money, a car, or any emotional support was tough. I relied heavily on the people who were placed in my life who were also in recovery. I realized I was capable of much more than I had previously given myself credit for. I learned that I am a hard worker who will do whatever it takes to rebuild my life.

Slowly but surely, I began to make a life for myself. Though progress was slow, each step reminded me that I had the strength to rebuild. At first, it felt like my decision to move had cost me everything, but later I found I would gain things I never even knew I wanted. The best perk of a location change is that you can create any kind of identity you want. No one in York has known me as anything but sober; here, I am reliable, trustworthy, and respected.

My new identity didn't come without struggles, of course. In my early recovery, my kids weren't talking to me, I was getting divorced, and my ex-husband started dating someone I knew. Newly sober, I was raw and vulnerable, overwhelmed by pain. In treatment, I often heard that drugs and alcohol weren't my problem, which was impossible to comprehend at the time. But when substances were removed from the equation, my problem became painfully clear: it was me. Drugs and alcohol were my temporary solutions. Because if drugs and alcohol are my problem, then without them, I should be fine, but that could not be farther from the truth. Once they were gone and I was left alone, the real problems began. The real problems are all my unresolved mental health issues, my PTSD, my lack of self-worth, and self-esteem.

At this critical juncture, fear consumed me. I realized that every decision I made in life was driven by my two biggest fears: not being good enough and being alone. This insight hit me hard, but it was the first step toward understanding myself. I was a people pleaser with no idea who I was, so I started liking whatever my friends or dates liked. Surprisingly, this feeling of insecurity played a role in one of the most important days of my life. Stressed after a bad dating experience, I called my sponsor, who asked me, "What did you learn?" Stumped, I challenged her to answer the question. I stated, "I don't know Sarah, what did we learn?" The following statement would change my life forever. She replied, "When are you going to stop being who you think everyone else wants you to be and just be the woman that you were meant to be?"

At that moment, I had no idea who that woman was, but I've worked hard to find out ever since. I no longer try to make myself smaller to fit in any relationship, whether romantic, friendly, or professional. If you don't like me, that's okay, because I like me. My personality can be very polarizing, but I don't lose any sleep over it because I know I have fought hard to become the woman I am today.

I started working in treatment when I reached one year of sobriety. Almost immediately, I found the same passion and purpose I had felt while I was in the military. I realized that helping others in recovery allowed me to serve something bigger than myself, something I truly believed in. I began as a third-shift detox technician and then became a case manager. However, I knew my ultimate goal was to be a counselor, so I had a decision to make.

Remember that fear I had of not being good enough? That fear kept me from going to college as a teenager. I didn't think I'd get accepted, so I never even applied. But in June 2020, I earned my bachelor's degree. This milestone was just the beginning; I continued my education, earning my master's and a PhD on the way. I achieved all of this because I finally figured out my purpose in life: to help as many people as possible who felt like I did, letting them know there is hope and that they can get better, too.

As a counselor, I used my own struggles to connect with clients on a deeply personal level, helping them navigate the challenges of recovery. My favorite moments were working with clients and seeing the light return to their eyes. I always considered myself a confrontational therapist, unafraid to address difficult truths with compassion. Because I have firsthand experience, I often use motivational interviewing techniques, encouraging clients to explore beyond surface-level responses.

One of the most important areas of my life that recovery has touched is my relationships, especially with my new husband. He guided me to my spiritual awakening and helped me become the woman I'm truly meant to be. I used to try to be the girl he thought I was, but he never asked me to change or tried to dim my light. He supports my goals, makes me feel safe, and has healed parts of me he didn't break. I don't need him—I simply want him in my life. He's my best friend, my authentic self shines with him, and he's also an incredible bonus parent to my children.

My relationship with my children was rocky at first, and, truthfully, it's still not always easy. I caused a lot of damage. My oldest, now twenty-five, had to grow up far too soon, stepping into a parent role when I couldn't. My daughter, now twenty, carries the memory of me lying on the bed like that—an image I can never erase. And my youngest, now seventeen, had to grieve the mom that he thought I was. I couldn't force my relationship with my kids; I learned that my family had to heal on their own time, not on my time. That meant that I showed up and was reliable. If I said I was going to call, I called, whether they answered the phone or not. If I said I was going to show up, then I was there. I had to show them that I was different by my actions, not my words. Although my relationship with my children is a work in progress and is far from perfect, I know they are all very proud of me and my recovery. They understand I am very open about my life, and they aren't embarrassed by that. Each of them has told me I'm one of the strongest people they know, which means more to me than they will ever understand.

Recovery has improved my relationship with my ex-husband as well. When he began dating his wife, I struggled. It was tough to see someone else care for my children when I couldn't. Now, I greatly appreciate her as a bonus mom, and let her know that regularly. What started as a competition has become a yin-and-yang relationship, with each of us balancing what we provide for the kids. The four of us co-parent together as a team, showing up for my children as a united front.

I have meaningful friendships with people today, and I laugh with them more than I ever thought possible. I never thought that I would be capable of having people in my life, but especially women who will show up for me when I need them. In sobriety, I've realized that I'm capable of being a friend and of receiving friendship in return.

A few pivotal moments in my recovery completely changed my perspective on life. I once carried deep resentment for the trauma I endured, but I've since found purpose in all that pain. Without purpose, we're left with nothing but pain. I've come to believe that everything I experienced happened for a reason: to prepare me to help others navigate similar struggles.

Finding purpose in my pain was a turning point, but understanding that purpose required me to take full responsibility for my recovery and embrace the hard work ahead. I realized that I couldn't control the negative things that happened to me, but if I chose to stay in that darkness, it would be my fault. No one else could decide to get better for me; I had to do it myself. Through this process, I shifted from seeing myself as a victim to recognizing myself as a survivor. As a victim, I give away all my power. But as a survivor, I reclaim that power and grow even stronger. I no longer feel defeated by the people who doubt me. When someone tells me I can't do something, I use it as fuel for my fire and say, "Watch me."

What keeps me sober today is knowing that I have another relapse in me; I don't know if I have another recovery in me. This awareness drives me to protect everything I've worked so hard to achieve, a life more beautiful than I could have dreamed. I no longer run from my past or wish to shut the door on it. Every experience—the good, the bad, and the ugly—has shaped me into the woman I am today. I'm not just a survivor; I'm someone capable of creating positive change, helping others find their way out of the darkness. I'm forever grateful to those who helped me find my way out, and I'll keep a light on for those who are still lost.

Time takes time. What I mean is that, of course, I wanted to heal immediately; I want to be better immediately. And what I have realized now is that there are parts of me that may truly never be healed. The memories of the assaults will come up out of the blue, whether it is a smell or a sound that brings back those feelings, but what has changed is how I deal with them. I allow myself to feel the emotions, but not get lost in them. I have been to therapy off and on for years. I strongly believe that this is a journey that will last a lifetime for me. I am not sure that I will ever truly be healed, but with therapy, my twelve-step program, love from my husband, family, and friends, I will continue to do the work to heal and realize that I am a continuous work in progress.

Jessica Osborn, MS, CAADC, CRS, CCTP

Jessica Osborn, Certified Advanced Alcohol and Drug Counselor, Certified Recovery Specialist, and Certified Clinical Trauma Professional, is a committed mental health advocate with a unique blend of personal and professional experience. A nine-year veteran of the United States Air Force, Jessica draws on her resilience and determination to help others overcome challenges.

Her own battle with addiction has shaped Jessica's journey. Since achieving sobriety, she has earned a bachelor's and master's degree and is currently pursuing a Ph.D. in Psychology with a specialization in substance-related and addictive disorders.

Jessica has worked in the substance use field since 2018, leveraging her experience as a dual-diagnosis patient and her successful recovery from addiction to provide compassionate care. She is dedicated to serving her community, believing her life's purpose is to help others find theirs.

"The fact that you are a victim is not your fault; the fact that you stay a victim is." –Jessica Osborn

CHAPTER 4

A Journey from Darkness to Redemption
Dennis Hannan

I didn't grow up with the goal of becoming an alcoholic or a drug addict. No one really does. My childhood was set against the backdrop of a home where alcohol was not only permitted but encouraged. The clinking of glasses, the laughter, the easy camaraderie – these were the sounds and sights that filled my early years. I loved everything about alcohol, especially how it made me feel comfortable in my own skin. It was liquid courage that made me feel attractive and funny. Alcohol had transformed me into the life of the party. Until it didn't. Until I couldn't imagine life without it, and drinking became all that mattered.

My earliest recollections of growing up around alcohol are of my mother waking me and my siblings in the middle of the night, or early morning, running down a laundry list of drinks she had consumed that night, from Golden Cadillacs to Pink Squirrels. She sometimes would have twigs and leaves in her hair from all the falls she took while walking home from the bar. She was a member of a club where you had to be buzzed in. It was a world that enthralled, intrigued, and eluded me during my youth. It all sounded glamorous, and I wanted to be a part of that world. I needed to be part of that world.

Deep down, even from a young age, I knew I had an addictive personality. I think my first addiction was Elvis Presley. Since the age of four, I have been a huge fan, learning everything I could about him, including memorizing his mannerisms and movements on stage. When Elvis died two days before my tenth birthday in 1977, you would have thought a member of the family had died. Relatives were calling the house to check on me. I cried for three straight days. Also, to this day, I still try to perfect Elvis's movements and style.

As the youngest child of seven, I looked forward to my siblings getting married because I could drink as much as I wanted for free at their weddings. Three brothers and two sisters were married before I was of legal age to drink, but by this time, I was a seasoned veteran.

I learned very early in life that there was a hierarchy when it came to my mother's favorites; I was last in line for her attention. You had to earn her affection. The smarter or more athletic you were, the prouder my mother was of you. I so wanted my mother's approval; however, eventually, I lost any illusions I had about rising in the ranks. When I was in grade school, I made the varsity basketball team, and instead of congratulating me or saying she was proud of me, the only words my mother said were, "Just don't embarrass the family name." I had come to the obvious conclusion that I was looking for approval I would never receive.

High school was where my drinking took off. I was the ultimate "Weekend Warrior." My friends and I had a club. We called ourselves the S.U.D.S. Club, which many knew meant beer, but we gave ourselves the acronym "Students Under Disciplinary Sanctions." Brilliant, right? The only rule my parents had for me was, "If you get arrested, don't call us." I am not sure how, but I was not arrested, not yet anyway. That came later.

I took one of my finals in my senior year completely drunk. I nearly missed the exam because I was out the night before, drinking with my friends who were in the graduating class the year before me. How I passed that test and graduated is beyond me. I wasn't a bad student; I just didn't have my priorities in the correct order. While most of my friends grew up, got married, started families and careers, I was stuck, merely existing. I bounced from job to job while living at home with no direction in life.

At twenty-four, I took a significant step into adulthood – I got married and soon after, became a father to a beautiful daughter. For many, such milestones are a wake-up call to maturity and responsibility, but I was not ready to give up the so-called "single life." I wanted the party to continue. I tried to hit the bars each night with people who wanted to drink and party as much as I did. From drinking "Mega Mugs" of beer for Monday Night Football to Thursday night karaoke bars, the weekends were made for not coming home. I wanted to keep partying and find anyone who wanted to do the same. For me, being a husband and a father was not enough to curb the growing grip of alcohol. My wife at the time, who had waited patiently for me to grow up, had finally had enough. She left, taking our daughter with her. Oddly, I felt a sense of relief. Her departure meant I could drink without pretense or apologies. I was free to do as I wanted, without repercussions or arguments. I had arrived. I was living on my own, going out every night, without a care or responsibility in the world. How stupid I was.

By the age of thirty, I found myself remarried, this time to someone who introduced me to the world of drugs. I was immediately hooked. The following two years were a blur – another daughter was born, and another marriage ended in divorce. It seemed that every time I tried to rebuild, my addictions would bulldoze through my life, leaving nothing but debris.

Once again, I was on my own, free to live my life. I made feeble attempts at sobriety. I went to rehab to appease the people who remained in my life, which were few.

Late in November of 2000, I was pulled over near my home and charged with a DUI after a police officer noticed I took a turn "a little wide." I thought it was a fluke, and I was just the victim of bad luck. A week later, I received a second DUI and spent the weekend in jail.

Desperate to get away as soon as I was released, I hopped on a Greyhound bus and left for Florida with literally just the clothes on my back. I had started a relationship with a woman who I knew would jump at the chance to have a man, any man, really, give her attention. Once again, I took another hostage because she enabled my behavior and put a roof over my head. I took advantage of situations and made them fit my lifestyle and purpose at that time. I preyed on the low self-esteem of others and used that to my advantage by telling them what I knew they wanted to hear, such as "you're too pretty to be alone," or "you are the perfect person!"

A few months later, I went back home for a family reunion. The morning after I flew in, there was a knock on the door. It was the police. I had warrants out for my arrest, and they wasted no time putting me into custody. I never made the reunion, and I do not know if my relatives had any idea I was in jail. I spent two months in prison before being released, and had my probation transferred to Florida. I was a model citizen until probation ended.

By this time, my family had just given up on me. To them, I was an embarrassment and a failure as a person. I had been the only person in my family to be arrested and go to jail. Using drugs was the ultimate disgrace in the eyes of my family, and they wanted as much space between them and me as possible. They washed their hands of me, and I washed my hands of them.

Where I lived in Florida was the New York Mets Spring Training home. When the minor league team played, I was in the stands for every Thursday night home game. $1.00 admission, $1.00 hot dogs, and most importantly, $1.00 beers. I was in heaven. The beer vendors got to know me so well that they would charge me $3.00 for a large souvenir cup because the $1.00 cups were too small. I felt like royalty.

Less than a year after I moved to Florida, one of my brothers died by suicide. I did not have a close relationship with him. I attributed his death to the result of a life of drinking. His death, however, was not a deterrent to my drinking. I thought I was "stronger" than my brother, and alcohol and drugs. I flew home for the funeral, and then went back to my life in Florida, as out of control as it was. Looking back, I wish I could have been there for my brother. I knew that because I wasn't sober, I could not have helped him, but now that I am sober, my wish is that I knew then what I know now. That there was a way out. That making a permanent solution to a temporary problem was not the answer. Life would get better. Unfortunately, I do not have the luxury of time travel, and hindsight is 20/20. I do, however, have continued contact with my two nieces, nephew, and sister-in-law, and try to be a pillar of hope for them as a tribute to my brother. I do miss him, and I love him. I wish I had told him that while he was alive.

Somewhere along the line, my girlfriend got pregnant, and she told me that my child would not have my name if I did not marry her. No big deal, I married her to keep her "happy" and continued my spiral. Just a couple of days after we were married, we had a daughter. To this day, I have no clear idea of what date I was married. This was another example of me "escaping" from the real world of responsibility to keep my lifestyle intact. My careless behavior then was unfair to my wife and to the daughter I had brought into this world. Both deserved better than what I was offering, which was nothing.

In the fall of 2003, my father had a stroke, and it was just him and my mother at home. I moved my family back to Pennsylvania to help my mother. In actuality, it was free room and board. More money for drinking! My wife and I gradually grew apart mainly due to my drinking and because of her disdain for Pennsylvania. She wanted the warmth and climate of Florida, so she took our daughter and moved back. By the time I was thirty-six, I had been divorced three times, I had no steady job, no relationship with any of my daughters, and my family wanted nothing to do with me.

I found another partner, another enabler, another hostage, another person I relied upon for everything – food, shelter, even my self-worth. Deep down inside, I felt completely inadequate. She seemed to have her life together. I wanted to be better, but the pull of addiction was too strong. For the next fourteen years, I spiraled into a dark abyss. I was arrested numerous times, in and out of rehabs and mental institutions, along with several weak suicide attempts. I didn't want to die, but at the same time, I did not want to go on living. My existence became a cycle of dependency and despair.

My partner's best idea to stop my drinking and drugging was to lock me in the basement for a year and only provide me with three meals a day. I actually thought this was a good idea! She also said that she would not marry me until I had at least one year of sobriety. That wasn't much of an incentive, having already been divorced three times. There were times when she went away for work, and I took this as my time to do what I wanted. Each time she came home, she would open the door to an empty house and just say to herself, "Oh no, not again." For whatever reason, she did not give up on me. She went to Al-Anon, and I drifted in and out of Alcoholics Anonymous.

As I neared fifty, I heard through the grapevine that I had become a grandfather. It was a jarring realization, but it didn't spur an immediate change. I had resigned myself to the belief that dying in the throes of addiction was my fate. And so, I tried, again and again to reach that final end.

Nothing outside of myself could stop me. I was on a path of self-destruction, barreling towards oblivion with no brakes in sight. They say that death isn't the worst thing that will happen to you – it's just the last thing.

Then, something truly miraculous happened. It was an ordinary day that started like any other, with me setting out for what I thought would be another run towards death. But fate intervened. As I drove, the road I usually took was closed. It's a road that would be closed during heavy rain because it floods. To block the road, a railroad-style crossing barrier would be lowered, cutting off access. On this day, there was no rain; there was no flood. As a matter of fact, there was not a cloud in the sky. However, due to a malfunctioning crossing barrier that had been lowered and blocked the road, I could not proceed. I could have taken another route, but for some reason, I didn't.

Something deep inside me spoke – a quiet voice that I had ignored for so long. It said, "You really don't want to do this anymore." I could no longer live the life I was living, and I certainly could not do it by myself. It was a simple yet profound decision. That moment marked the beginning of my journey towards recovery. I turned the car around, drove to Brooke Glen Behavioral Hospital, and asked for help. There, I met a therapist named Dr. Patrick McElwaine who changed my life. "Dr. Mac" made a lasting impact on me that I carry with me to this day. He saw something in me that I couldn't see in myself. Dr. Mac saw me as a person with empathy, kindness, and a true desire to not only help myself, but also to help others. Most importantly, Dr. Mac saw a person and looked past the disease. Dr. Mac had a saying in the group that I repeat every day: "Don't be an asshole." Simple, yet powerful. If I am not an asshole to people, they most likely won't be an asshole towards me.

For the first time in my life, I fully embraced a twelve-step recovery program. I immersed myself in everything it had to offer. I got a sponsor, and I worked the steps. Slowly, my life improved. The chaos that had defined my existence settled, and a new sense of purpose emerged. I started a career in commercial insurance. Now, if I leave a job, it's because I want to, not because my employer is tired of the endless excuses that used to come up every Monday after payday.

I am now married to the woman who has watched my ups and downs for over twenty years. Together, we are building a life filled with meaning and joy. Everything I had lost is slowly being restored. My daughters are back in my life, and I have the incredible gift of being a grandfather.

Before my mother-in-law passed away, we had formed a relationship built on trust and love. This was a woman who once stood in my living room and called me "a worthless piece of shit." At the time, she was right. I was. After being sober for a few years, she saw that I was someone she could rely on without any ulterior motives. We realized we had more in common than we didn't. We both loved going on little adventures and meeting celebrities. We had fun when we were together, and I am forever grateful for having her as my mother-in-law.

The best gift I ever gave my own mother was that when she died, I was sitting beside her sober. All my mother really wanted for me was to be sober and happy. It took me a lifetime to figure this out. She died knowing I was both of those things. I have also mended years of separation and non-communication with my brothers and sisters. They now see a man who finally "grew up." A man who keeps his word and is dependable. I am now invited to weddings for my nieces and nephews without them being afraid I will get drunk and act the fool, which I had often done. I can joke with my siblings today by saying I liked it better when they didn't talk to me because I was never invited to anything, and didn't have to spend so much money.

Speaking of money … I now have a bank account that is on the positive side. I no longer worry about whether my bills will get paid or if my phone will be shut off. I was able, for the first time in my life, to purchase a brand-new truck in my name. My wife and I had a plan to get out of debt within three years. At the time, we had over $60,000 in student loan debt, payments on a new truck, and a $100,000 home equity loan. As of this printing, we are 100% debt-free. My wife has a new car as well, which is also paid off. I am not saying money is the most important thing to success. To me, success means having people trust my word and know that I mean what I say. My children can rely on me for anything, and my grandchildren look forward to seeing me.

My life is by no means perfect. I have experienced the death of family and friends. I have had my first surgery ever and refused narcotic pain relievers. I have lost jobs in sobriety, but not because of my behavior. My youngest daughter still goes through bouts of not speaking to me. Not because of anything I have done, but rather because I have established boundaries and will not be a doormat because of the guilt I felt in the past.

Today, my story is one of hope and redemption. I am living proof that no matter how deep you've sunk, there is always a way out. My life is now a testament to the power of change, the strength of the human spirit, and the profound impact of finding a reason to keep going.

I was convinced my lot in life was to die homeless and penniless in the gutter. Asking for help is not a weakness. Asking for help is the first step in regaining your life. Just doing the "next right thing" and the "right thing next," life becomes much easier to manage. I no longer have to remember what story I told to whom. My story remains the same as long as I am honest with myself and all those around me.

I share my story not just as a personal recount, but as a beacon for anyone who feels hopeless. If I can find my way back from the brink, so can you. This is my journey – from the depths of addiction to the heights of a life reclaimed and one that is constantly evolving.

Dennis Hannan

Dennis Hannan is from the streets of Philadelphia, literally. Dennis came into the world on a hot summer day in the family car, on the way to the hospital at 22nd and Passyunk Avenue in South Philadelphia. He is the youngest of seven children of an Irish-Catholic family.

Dennis graduated from Bishop Kenrick High School in 1985 and began working in insurance in 1989. In 2005, he became a matriculated college student and received his associate degree in 2008 at the age of forty. Dennis currently works in the commercial insurance industry.

Dennis is married to his fourth wife, lives in the Philadelphia suburbs, and has three beautiful daughters and five amazing grandchildren: four boys and one girl. Dennis feels truly blessed.

CHAPTER 5

The Gift of Desperation
Alison Gontowski

I can't even pick what kind of outfit I want or how I wear my hair or where I want to have my birthday party - I wonder how it's so easy for the kids around me? I can't decide if I like vanilla or chocolate, or what I want to be when I grow up, or what sport I want to play. I don't know which school subject is my favorite, I just like the one where the teacher thinks I do a good job. I just want to choose whatever makes me good in your eyes.

From a young age, I remember a few core feelings. I craved acceptance and validation. I was insecure. I longed to stay home and not leave. When I did have to go, I wanted so badly to fit in and to be liked by teachers, parents, and peers. It was terrifying and exhausting. I remember having an overwhelming urge to be perfect, even as I knew I never would be. I remember a feeling of such awkwardness that I was sure others could see how I felt. I remember having anxiety about my looks, my actions, and being convinced that my internal dialogue was irrefutably *real*. Inside and out, I was ugly; everyone pitied me, and I was hopeless. I wanted the courage to know what I wanted, how to ask for it, and the comfort I thought I would come to feel if someone told me exactly what I was supposed to do. I wanted to feel free, but I didn't know what freedom was.

As I got older, I avoided sleepovers. I would have meltdowns if I didn't get A's. I believed something was wrong with me: physically, mentally, or emotionally, and people just weren't telling me. As normal adolescent teasing commenced, I would hear those criticisms and etch them in my mind as if they were gospel. Being made fun of for stuttering while giving a presentation in front of class and having someone "baaaahhh" like a billy goat? Yep, that stuck with me and ended up on my fourth step list decades later. Being picked on for my tone-deaf and beat-late singing? Yep, that resulted in a disproportionate reaction, too, when I decided the only acceptable response was never to sing out loud again. Through my recovery, I would learn I was carrying these criticisms as resentments. Breaking it down further, I'd discover that many of those resentments were rooted in my ego and fed by my fears.

I adapted to my insecurities through defense mechanisms. I started watching the people around me and learning from what they did and how they acted, writing my invisible rule book of "What Normal Looks Like" by Alison. I remember a supervisor calling me a "chameleon," and I received that title as a badge of honor. I learned that if I tucked an insecurity away and spit it back out as confidence, I could fool everyone around me. Through trial and error, I found a way of life that worked for me. This way of life was one in which I portrayed myself as having everything under control. If I could convince the people who love me that I was doing GREAT, it would bring them joy. I became addicted to achieving. By earning high grades, working multiple jobs, being an athlete, and finding a relationship, I had plenty of evidence to prove how great I was. The additional bonus was how busy it kept me, so I never had to sit alone with myself.

I threw my shoulders back, put a smile on my face, and people seemed to like me better. When I tried to be honest about not being okay and the façade slipped, it felt like people avoided me until I was joyful and easy again. In recovery, I've recognized that this projection of confidence, while it may have protected me at times, was also a form of manipulation. I manipulated the people around me, and at the root of it all, I manipulated myself. Almost immediately, I recognized alcohol allowed me to flip the switch and shut down my insecurities—and to let my ego come out to play. I would sing, and dance, and talk your ear off. I didn't need to be in control, and the smile that spread across my face felt so effortless. I was no longer a bundle of nervous energy, hiding my thousand forms of fear. I was bold and loud and most of the time, charming. Sometimes I'd get sloppy, but I'd find an excuse for any situation—I'd hide behind my accomplishments or my tragedies so you would ignore the gaping hole in the back of the crashing plane.

The first time I blacked out, I was intrigued rather than scared. During my blackouts, "Autopilot Ali" became a version of me who had confidence and lacked fear, which others gravitated toward. As people answered to "Autopilot Ali," it reinforced my decision to feel comfortable drinking the way my ego desired. I could live a double life of Ali during the day, and "Autopilot Ali" at night. Most mornings, I'd end up playing detective, piecing the clues of my life together, interviewing people I had been with, checking my pockets for receipts, and my phone (if it wasn't broken) for other evidence.

What mattered most to me after these evenings was whether anyone was mad at me. If the answer was no, everything else was tolerable. Scrapes or bruises? Battle scars. Spent more money than I had? That's the price I pay. Drove my car home? Lucky. Embarrassed myself and abandoned my daytime morals and ethics? Wasn't me—blame Autopilot Ali. What was my top priority? I needed people to believe I was as happy as I was portraying myself to be. I was terrified of being outed as the fraud I felt I was. As the days, weeks, and years went by, the web I spun only grew denser. I found more comfort in carrying my own burdens and avoiding negative attention. If I just kept forcing forward, I had to figure it out eventually, right?

In recovery, I learned that living a life of lies would never cure my addiction. No amount of accomplishments was going to fill the void in my soul. Life felt fast and out of control. Throughout my years in active addiction, I would graduate with a bachelor's degree, a master's degree, and start a Ph.D. program. I would serve honorably in the military for fourteen years. I would begin to and maintain a successful career in law enforcement. I would outperform many of my peers in terms of careers, grades, and social activities. I would serve on nonprofit boards and file my taxes on time. All the while, I would wake up most days disappointed that I was still alive.

I was suffering in silence, hiding behind a cloak of "I'm just having a good time." I would keep people at the precise distance I wanted, revealing only certain parts of my life to the people I could trust with the particular pieces. It was vitally important that no one got the whole picture. I thought myself the victim of the world around me. Over those twenty years, I lost my father to cancer and turned to an eating disorder. I faced arrest, spiraled into debt, and experienced disciplinary actions at work. I underwent multiple heart surgeries and hurt those closest to me with my words and actions. I made promises I genuinely intended to keep, only to break them almost immediately. I would be violated, and I would violate myself.

I would justify it all while feeling increasingly divided. I felt more and more like my insides didn't match my outsides. I used to refer to the feeling in my journal entries as "feeling like I'm wearing a human suit." Existence became utterly exhausting. I ended up convinced I was a bad person, even though I knew I wanted to be a good one. At a certain point, I believe I drank to "let loose." When I struggled to regulate myself emotionally, I think I started using drinking as an excuse and a vehicle to take back from the world that owed me. Over the years, that morphed into creating two versions of me—the drinking version that took actions in the dark, and the daytime version left sinking from the residual shame. I tried fighting against the weight of the shame, but over time, that narrative won, and I'd drink again to calm the self-hate inside my head.

I ended up in a place where I didn't feel I was deserving of love. I questioned the people around me who said they cared about me. I was convinced most people just pitied me. I thought so lowly of myself, but spent significant amounts of time trying to convince people to trust me, to love me, and to believe in me. Just like I was splitting in two, my ego did, too. One side was a martyr, the other invincible.

I grew to crave complication and ended up not trusting simple answers. I was used to lighting my own dumpster fires so that I could put them out. If I kept up the charade, the show would go on. I felt sure that not everyone thought the way I did, and I also believed there wasn't any other way for me to live. I developed a narrative that relying on a safety raft was weak, and my method of thrashing in the water was superior and safer. I would continue trying harder to control things and believed that if I put enough pressure on myself, I would succeed. I felt like I was firing on all cylinders, but none of them were working quite right. Rather than the pressure making me stronger, it made me progressively more fragile. I could run all day and all night, but I couldn't outrun feeling like I was teetering on the brink of breaking. It was such a frantic feeling, and alcohol was a ripcord I could pull to feel relief from what was happening inside me.

On October 12, 2019, I finally received the gift of desperation. I knew my way of life wasn't working, and if I didn't try something different, I didn't want to keep living. At that moment, I still begged for any solution other than giving up drinking. I called friends I thought would assure me

I was fine, and to my surprise, one told me I should try to stop drinking. My suffering had become great enough that I knew I didn't want to live like this anymore. Thankfully, I wasn't ready to die, so I followed the advice given to me, and I walked into a noon AA meeting. The chairperson at my first meeting said to me, "You never have to feel this way again," triggering a flood of tears. I'm not sure I believed him, but the words were so profound, I accepted them. I still repeat that phrase to other people who are still suffering. If only I had known then that by giving up one thing, I would gain everything.

In early recovery, I felt the highs and lows. I was feeling it all, and the intensity was heightened. I felt like a teenager, and in many ways, I still mentally was. In sobriety, I have developed emotionally, mentally, and spiritually the way many people do as teens and young adults. I faced hard facts head-on—like how I had spent my life wishing people to be perfect versions of themselves for me, while ignoring my own imperfections. I've been resistant to following suggestions, usually falling back on old habits of wanting to be the one steering the ship. Even though my sense of direction isn't the one I should be following. I've convinced myself I was doing good enough to "ease up" on the things I know help me, and I've ended up right back in Crazy Town. I've struggled with balance and extremist thinking. I struggle to reprogram my brain to stop thinking things are all-or-nothing. I'm either the best or I'm worthless. I'm either in control of everything or in control of nothing. I'm either going to the gym five days a week or avoiding it for years. Moderation has never been my strong suit. In recovery, I've worked hard to create a life based around things being "right-sized," something my sponsor encourages me to pay attention to. This thought process helps me strive for stability and to regulate myself. I give more power and value to the days I'd rate as average than I do to the outliers.

One struggle that I hung up on for a while was the topic of faith. I didn't think I believed in God, listing any reason I could come up with poverty, injustices, illnesses, tragic deaths, you name it. What recovery has taught me is that in my active resistance to God, I had been playing the role of my own god. I tried calling the shots; I tried managing the playbook.

After decades of trying that over and over, I came to realize … I'm pretty terrible at being God. I also realized I can't be mad at a God I don't believe in, so it's not that I didn't believe in him; I was just mad at him. I remained fiercely skeptical of the concept of religion and spirituality well through early sobriety. What was most helpful was admitting I did a terrible job at being the almighty controller of my entire life. The mathematician in me concluded that if what I was doing hadn't been working out so well, I had nothing to lose by trying it a different way. I found comfort in knowing I could always return to my old way of life, which was filled with chaos.

I went through a phase where I wanted to research every religion and thoroughly understand my options before choosing one. I struggled with the concept that if I turned control over to God, what was my job? My all-or-nothing mind kicked in just to try to prove this new way of thinking wrong. Hours of conversation, reading, talking, and overanalyzing led me to a point where I can draw a physical circle around myself. I envision what's inside the circle is still mine. What's outside the circle is not mine, and I don't necessarily need to know whose it is. That's where my spiritual journey started.

I still have a lot of discovering to do, but I know that ever since I fired myself from being God, my life has kept getting better.

Through committing myself to recovery, I've learned to rely on something other than myself. I have started to understand how I was contributing to my suffering, and how I still get in my own way today.

Recovery taught me I was seeking approval from bosses, my sponsor, and friends, without acknowledging they were also imperfect, flawed, and focused on their own lives. These people had their own insecurities, and most people in my life did not judge me as harshly as I judged myself. Recovery allowed me to make amends to family members for holding them to standards I wasn't holding myself to, to coworkers and supervisors I had disappointed, and to friends whom I had wronged while acting selfishly. Not all of those amends turned out the way I wanted, but they were freeing nonetheless. I got to accept the circumstances of my life and forgive the people and situations I resented. Once I reached that acceptance and forgiveness, I accepted and forgave myself. I opened my eyes to faults in myself I didn't want to see, and a beauty in others I was missing because of what I was holding on to. I get to attempt to clean up my messes, and I get to keep a cautious eye on myself for when my faults pop up.

The life I get to live today is one I'm afraid to lose, and that's something I didn't believe was real five years ago.

I now know I don't have a choice as to whether I am an alcoholic, whether I have an addicted brain. Once I admitted I was an alcoholic, the choice I was left with was whether I wanted to accept help or continue to suffer silently, paving a path of destruction. I have tried both options, and since I know the suffering, I will keep choosing to participate in my treatment. To get out of my head and into helping someone else. To check my ego with healthy doses of gratitude. To counter my fears, by re-grounding myself in the present. To stop being obsessed with what other people think of me and continue learning how to trust myself, my own decisions, and my own assessment of myself.

Life has become so much more fun now that I've gotten to know myself. Now that I am driven by what feels right to me, rather than what I think I should want. Now that I don't feel paralyzed by fear of judgment, rejection, and failure. Now that I try to make it a priority to just take one step in the right direction, over and over.

All I wanted was love, yet I spent many years thinking I wasn't worthy of it. Today, I know with every cell in my being, I am worthy of that love—that my insides finally match my outsides. Today, I get to do so much. I get to have a job where I help people every day. I get to continue to actively choose my wife and my marriage by being intentional with my time and making sure my efforts are meaningful to her. I get to take the vacation day to spend with her, even if it's just to drive to the beach for a day or take our dogs on a hike. I get to show up and be present in quality friendships. I get to show my family I love them. I get to put down the heavy weight of resentments that don't serve me. I get to pray. I get to ask for help, for guidance, and for courage. I get to reflect on these parts of my life and feel immense gratitude for them.

I'm nowhere near perfect, and that's why I try to focus on today. Sometimes I feel like I have an Etch-a-Sketch brain, and every day it's shaken back to a clean slate. Sometimes my internal narrative will take hold. When going for a promotion at work, I'm afraid I'm "not good enough" and can spiral with negative self-talk. If I forget to take care of a responsibility, I can spiral just as intensely. When I set a goal for myself like going to the gym, a certain number of days, or making better choices with my diet, and I don't reach the goal, I can be disproportionately hard on myself, feeling like I never should have tried in the first place. Being able to catch myself and run that spiral back to its root, which is usually fear. Then I allow myself to remember I'm human, and the best I can do is take corrective action and try to do better. I need to wake up each day and be willing to be free.

Willing to relinquish myself from the role of director and just be a person among people. Willing to remember that lovingly—I am not special. Willing to pay attention to my expectations, which are usually rooted in fear. Willing to face those fears with *acceptance*. Willing to check myself and make sure things are "right-sized," including my emotions, reactions, fears, and insecurities. Willing to tell on myself and to do my best to make it right when I mess up. Willing to stop bulldozing my life and understand I'd be better served by gentle pressure applied consistently. Willing to surrender, to give grace, and to give back. When I stay in varying degrees of willingness, I get to experience varying degrees of freedom.

Sometimes I catch myself looking back and wishing I had gotten to this place sooner than I did. Then I try to be thankful that I didn't sink into a deeper, darker desperation. I am grateful that today I woke up happy to be alive. I am proud of who I am and the life I live today. I focus on the fact that just for today, I get the chance to be a better version of myself.

Alison Gontowski

Alison Gontowski is a jack of many trades and a master of none. She has served in careers varying from waiting tables and tending bars to being a diesel mechanic and enforcing laws. Alison has enjoyed a lifelong love of reading and expressing herself through writing.

Based in Collingswood, NJ, Alison's journey in recovery has instilled a deep understanding of the importance of emotional well-being and balance in life, which she knows will likely be a forever work in progress. She attributes her ability to chase her many passions to the support she has from her wife, her family, and the family she has chosen through friendships and AA.

As a police officer, Alison not only excels in her professional duties but also prioritizes her own mental health and encourages others to do the same. Alison's commitment to emotional wellness is embodied through her professional and personal passions. In March of 2025, Alison was promoted to detective in the Special Victims Unit of the Abington Township Police Department.

CHAPTER 6

A Path to Wholeness: Becoming Me
Lisa Cordasco, MSW, LCSW, LCADC, CCS, CCTP, C-DBT, RYT-200

There are still moments that catch me off guard, where the world tilts for a pause, and I experience a wave of awe coming through my body. It ripples softly now, whereas in the past it would rumble through me, shaking my every cell. In those moments, I ask myself, "Is this really my life?"

Being a person in long-term recovery is an interesting experience. I've gotten to live multiple lifetimes in one. The past and present sometimes unravel, collide, and converge in the most surreal ways. "Yes," I whisper back to that child inside me—sometimes still fearful. "This is real—this IS life, and we are living it, we've worked hard, crawled out of the mud and fucking deserve it." And then I breathe.

I was nineteen years old when I got and stayed clean, just a few weeks before my 20th birthday in the fall of 2006. Although I didn't stay clean directly after my first attempt, the seeds were planted. I am one of the lucky ones who has gotten to walk through the flames and not only survive but thrive. The path of recovery and deep healing has been rocky, to say the least. A nineteen-year-old kid doesn't enter recovery because it seems like a fun thing to do—I was desperate. I was out of options; alone and petrified.

My final run landed me in Lake Worth, Florida, a kid from Jersey, completely out of place but still fully able to scope out where the drugs and underbelly were. I showed up to rehab in the dead of summer, with my leather combat boots held together with duct tape as my only footwear. 'Out of place' was an understatement. But sure enough, I linked up with a fresh romance (or two—the way I often did, preferring to keep both a female and male running partner on hand) and still believed in the idea that I had control or that I could 'figure it out on my own.' Although I had been introduced to the concept of accepting help and support from others in recovery, it was absolutely terrifying. I approached it with my typical guarded and skeptical nature. I was smarter and stronger. I could do it alone. But underneath all that bravado was the simple reality that, up until that point, life had done me dirty when it came to trust and relationships. Explaining this requires me to back up a bit.

We learn our value system early in life. We take in both overt and covert messaging from our environment about ourselves and the world around us. Much of my messaging was conflicting and confusing. A significant portion of my messaging was rooted in shame and mistrust. And, like children often do, I internalized it. I soaked it in, like thirsty soil in the rain.

I have pictures of myself as a child—not many, but a few—of me in beautiful frilly dresses or denim skirts, with my long hair streaked with gold from the sun and my skin tan and glowing. My eyes in these pictures are dark, like two black pools. And in some, you can see how I'm somewhere far away from the moment the shutter snapped.

Growing up with a parent with untreated severe mental health and substance use disorders impacted me greatly. Before my recovery journey, I didn't understand childhood trauma, intergenerational trauma, attachment wounds, or any of that. I didn't come to understand dissociation, disorganized attachment, anxiety disorders, emotional dysregulation, and the connection to my somatic struggles and autoimmune disorders for quite some time. When I look at those pictures now, I feel compassion for that little girl. I do not blame anyone for my addiction. I have compassion for my parents, their parents, and their ancestors. I acknowledge both that they did the very best they could with what they had, and their own unhealed parts showed up and got in the way. I love them for what they gave me and what they have taught me on this journey. I also acknowledge that many of my early experiences caused significant harm to my nervous system, my brain, my body, and my soul.

My memory of childhood is hazy at best. I didn't learn that exposure to chronic and prolonged stress and trauma, especially in early childhood, impacts a person's memory until years into my recovery. It actually changes the size and function of some brain regions, such as the hippocampus (which helps us store memory). I don't have a clear recollection of milestone events or details on an orderly timeline. When you click the 'play' button on the reel, rather than clearly projecting the story, the reel stutters, skips, freezes, and races uncontrollably. So, instead, I'm left with a cluster of sensations in my body, snapshots of fragmented scenes, waves of overwhelming sensory information, and the core beliefs internalized through those chronic patterns of behavior.

I believed for the first half of my life that relationships with other people were dangerous and conditional. That love had to be earned through performance, through sacrificing my own boundaries, needs, and feelings, and even then, it could be retracted or used against me. I believed I was responsible for others' emotions, and my own were irrelevant. I thought that there was something deeply unworthy and ugly inside of me, something that needed to be killed off or at least hidden if that wasn't possible.

Very early on, I learned the survival tactics of secrecy and hiding in plain sight, and often this created the fragmented experience of a double life. If I could just get small, become invisible, or play the part required until the danger subsided, everything would be okay. When you grow up with a caregiver who is consumed by their own unhealed pain, trauma, mental illness, and substance use issues, that becomes crucial.

A strong sense of instability and fear characterized my early life. Everything looked fine on the outside, but I knew I was walking across a loaded minefield daily. A joyful event—a birthday, holiday, success at school or work—could turn sour or downright catastrophic if the footing across that field weren't just right. The rules were invisible and unspoken, but the air always hung thick with expectation—the next storm always on the horizon. The small mistakes that every child undoubtedly makes were amplified to the level of a crime. Love, affection, and praise could be offered, and I'd gobble those morsels up when they were, but then quickly withdrawn or replaced by the acidic sting of shame or rejection. It became safer to keep my own needs tucked away inside and quiet. I learned to sense others' needs, moods, and shifts, and to morph the image I mirrored back to fit them. I became hypervigilant, perfectionistic, and deeply codependent. But there was also constant rewriting of history; my truth, feelings, or experiences were always distorted through the other person's lens, to the point where everything looked like a funhouse mirror. I even questioned the legitimacy of my feelings and thoughts.

I found ways to soothe the chaos and confusion that grew inside me. I hid my obsessive and compulsive traits and rituals. The one I clung to most was spelling out the letters of words as people were speaking them. I could see the letters in front of my eyes, and focusing on them soothed me and allowed me to remain a detached observer. There were also things I had to do because if I didn't, 'something bad' would happen. So,

I'd spell the letters. Or count, but only to specific numbers that were soothing, while others created more distress. Or touch things evenly, such as both sides of my body in the same way. That would make it all better. This also evolved into compulsive picking of the skin on my fingers, and later, my first addiction, self-injury.

I don't want to paint a picture of it all being bad. There were glimmers of hope, moments where I could catch my breath. There were even good times amid the chaos. My safe place was always nature, the ocean, and the woods. I would sit high in the trees for hours, building my own little world. I was also an artist and a seeker, a bit of a strange kid. I'd read books on ancient religion and mythology; I fell in love with Dali, O'Keeffe, Plath, and Poe. I got into punk and riot grrrl music, idolizing the freedom and wildness of the artists' expression. I began teaching myself to meditate at around eleven years old (not coincidentally), shortly after I first attempted suicide. There was always a small piece of me that knew there had to be hope, that was searching for being untethered from the pain I was holding inside. But then there were times when the darkness would swallow me up completely. I couldn't see through the muck and became terrified that the light I thought I had seen was just a mirage.

My body began attacking itself in early adolescence. It started with migraines at ten, and later the pain continued to spread. I had to quit gymnastics, the only space where I could be present within myself and feel my body underneath me. The pain began seeping into my muscles and bones, gripping me like hateful tentacles. It wasn't until years later that my body entirely refused to function, and I was diagnosed with several autoimmune disorders. By then, I had lost the will to fight against it.

Around age twelve, I began using substances. Alcohol had always been present in my life. It was a way to celebrate, cope, escape, and connect—

it was a normalized way of life. I joined in and immediately understood why that cabinet always stayed stocked. It dulled the sharp edges. I'd drink just enough not to be noticed before school each day, and more on the weekends. But when I found weed, that was even better. The pain in my body quieted, and I could laugh—oh God, I could laugh. It felt beautiful. I would do anything for that feeling of relief and a glimpse of joy. The first time I sold myself for substances was for weed. I was fourteen and needed to escape.

And we know how this story progresses, don't we? The world of prescription pills opened to me, offering all kinds of new and interesting ways to alter my mind, find that pressure relief valve, and pretend to be someone else, somewhere else. Hallucinogens continued on my road to spiritual seeking, though none of it seemed to bring me what I was looking for. I was the tortured artist, and I embraced it fully, immersing myself in it.

It was in my junior year of high school that the progression skyrocketed. I linked up with my first real running partner, Scott, whose life was taken years later—a risk that comes with the lifestyle, but tragic nonetheless. We fed the sickest, darkest, and most broken parts of one another, called it love, and fueled it with drugs. Cocaine sure is a hell of a drug, as is heroin, and the needle opened an ecstasy I hadn't known before. The warmth and soothing I experienced from shooting heroin is what I had been searching for. All the noise quieted, and everything was right with the world while I was drifting in that opiate embrace. By senior year, I focused all my time on getting high. I had manipulated my way onto a home-based schooling schedule because of my health issues, which allowed me to get a whole week's work done in a matter of hours— thanks to genetics and my perfectionistic conditioning. This gave me time to focus on using and obtaining the means to dope and coke. Being a young woman made it easy enough, and my years detaching from my physical body made it even easier.

I maintained high honors and received a scholarship to a fine arts college in Philadelphia. I convinced myself I could keep up the illusion that everything was okay, even with a raging addiction. I had learned to wear whatever masks were necessary, but by this time, even those masks began to crack. I had worked hard to maintain those old expectations of academic success and compliance, but the pain kept bubbling to the surface and was about to all bubble over. The double life was no longer sustainable.

Moving to Philadelphia and having unrestrained freedom was gasoline on the fire that was already flaming. Philly was an open playground—drugs were more easily accessible, available, and cheaper than I had ever known. And with the anonymity of being in a new place, the pressure to maintain an appearance that I had it together quickly fell away. My time in that city soon became filled with humiliation and shame. I'd puke in the bushes outside of class when I did show up, but mostly, I just didn't. My classmates and teachers saw what a strung-out mess I was, but I had no energy left to care. I wouldn't answer the phone for anyone in my family or my friends from before. I'd drive around Northeast Philadelphia until 3 a.m. smoking crack with strangers I'd met at the club, playing with some gang member's loaded gun, and making money with men old enough to be my grandfather. My relationships were a disaster. No one could stand me, and I couldn't stand myself. Everything was volatile, and I felt such intense abandonment and rejection that there wasn't enough heroin on the East Coast to ease the flames. I was both burning alive and freezing to death at once—I felt everything and nothing.

When I was arrested, it blew the lid off any remaining denial. My 'Tony Pop', the senior partner of a prestigious law firm, a war hero, and my personal idol, rescued me from my impending legal doom. I had gotten myself into a mess of a situation involving a stolen car, false police reports, and, of course, possession of drugs and paraphernalia. The arresting detective must have taken pity on me because she put my whopping 85lb self into the children's holding cell rather than in with the general population. I was a sobbing mess waiting for bail to be posted. As much as I may have thought I looked the part of someone tough with multicolored hair, chains, and pleather, I was just a lost and terrified kid. Tony Pop had already lost the relationship with one child due to the estrangement caused by addiction. He never said a word about it and quietly cleaned up my mess, but knowing I had disappointed him and brought up a familiar hurt was crushing.

I ended up in handcuffs again when I was apprehended during my final suicide attempt. We hadn't been able to score yet that day, so I was dope sick and miserable. Something in my relationship triggered those old, deep feelings of being completely unlovable, pushing my mood over the edge. I decided it was best to give death another shot. I didn't expect my partner to come home and call 911. Sirens blared, and I panicked. I remember being consumed with the need to hide under the bushes outside and die like a sick cat. I jumped out a window, wrists still bleeding, and staggered my way across the lawn of the apartment complex, when the 300lb cop responding to the 911 call tackled me, trying to get cuffs on despite the blood, while I thrashed underneath, screaming "just let me die". Shortly after, I failed out of school. I had lost my scholarship. I had overdosed countless times, and I was angry to wake up with each one. I told myself that I couldn't even die correctly. Rehab started to sound like a good idea. I was tired.

Rehab exposed me to a different possibility for my life. While I was there, a tiny shimmer of light, which I believed I had snuffed out, reignited. I didn't know that other people thought and felt how I did. I didn't know that people used drugs, but then stopped using and actually recovered. A tiny voice inside whispered, "Maybe me."

I still had a few more lessons to learn. I was afraid and distracted when I got out of treatment. I didn't know how to be alone, and I was drawn back to the bright lights of validation and easy money, thinking I could do what I had for money and attention in the past and stay clean this time. I felt a magnetic pull toward other broken people, hoping we could fill each other's wounded spaces. But healing doesn't work that way. I relapsed, and the bottom I thought I hit dropped out further. I found myself in utter desperation, worse off than I had been before.

That relapse was short, but brutal. Those last few days of using are seared into the folds of my brain. I see myself in that dirty motel room, turning myself into a human pincushion, sick, pleading to the stained ceiling and flickering lights to either let me get one good vein, one good hit, or to just put me out of my misery and let me die already.

The last time I overdosed, I heard the voice of a greater being, my Higher Power, in my own head. It may sound wild, but it saved me. My boyfriend, who later became my daughter's father, and I got the romantic notion of doing some speedballs and watching the sunrise on the beach. Michael decided he'd put both our shots in one syringe, and while we stood in the dirty beach bathroom, he reminded me only to push half. The plunger got stuck, and when I gave it a little extra force, I pushed the whole thing by mistake. I only remember hearing him say, "Fuck, you're going out on me, aren't you?" and then a sense of stillness and calm. A voice I had never heard before said simply, "Get into the ocean." Somehow, I relayed this to him, and he carried me into the cold waves. He held my nearly lifeless body, and we let the chilled waves hit me in the face. I lived. This was back when heroin was still heroin and not fentanyl. But the moment was profound in my journey. Something wanted me to live, even though I didn't seem to care about my own life.

It was a glimmer of hope. I used it for another week or two after that before I was ready to believe in hope, and an intervention came.

My mother, back in New Jersey, whom I had been avoiding at all costs for those weeks, got a call from her sister in California—someone I hadn't seen in years, a highly intuitive and spiritual woman who had introduced me to yoga. She told my mother, "Lisa is going to die if you don't go get her now." My mother informed me she was coming down to bring me back to New Jersey. I was both terrified and relieved.

I kicked on that motel floor. I crawled from the bed to the toilet like a dying animal. Michael wasn't done and continued to use it in the next room. But something in me snapped, and I decided that had to be it. I was no stranger to pain, so I let myself feel every exploding cell, every excruciating bit of that detox. I had to let myself feel it all. I think on some level, I had to really understand what I was doing to myself to find the courage to finally be ready to do something about it.

I came back to New Jersey with my tail between my legs, still shaking. But this time, I was willing to plead for and accept help.

I admitted I was scared and had no idea what to do. Gradually, I began to learn how to form trusting relationships and be part of a real community. I found the family and support I needed in the twelve-step community. I did a lot of deep work on myself. A lot. I had to face my demons and learn that those broken parts of me weren't actually the monsters I thought they were.

It took years to find a real sense of peace, but I kept believing it was possible. I never thought I had been lovable until my experiences with recovery. A pattern of secret keeping and hiding stayed with me for years. It took me almost five years into recovery to tell a single being about the sexual trauma I experienced early on. It took me longer to finally address it in therapy. And it took over a decade to get genuine relief in my body and to know what it was like to feel safe within my own self. I often say that the relationship with my sponsor was the first real, genuine, honest, and authentic relationship I had with another person. She, along with a small group of others, gave me a sense of safety I had been craving. In early recovery, I was afraid to hang out with other young people or those who were also early in recovery. I was fortunate enough to be scooped up by those "old timers", a number of whom I've buried, clean, over the years and miss deeply. They accepted me authentically while also nudging me forward, pushing me to do the work to get better.

I learned how to heal my mind, body, and soul. I made mistakes along the way, but most importantly, I didn't use. I just kept asking for and accepting the love and support I had craved for so long, often learning that I had to turn within myself to really find it.

That's not to say that in recovery I haven't experienced plenty of tragedy—losses that brought me to my knees and broke my heart to pieces. And yet, I'm grateful for the lessons those losses brought me. Like the loss of my best friend since age ten, Khushali—the only friend I retained through all the chaos. She was an alcoholic and I, a heroin addict—I still can't make it make sense that she died, and I got to live. But I know how precious life is and the importance of living each day to the fullest without leaving things unsaid.

I've had to make tough decisions, like choosing to jump headfirst into single motherhood at age twenty-two, (Michael still had his own lessons to learn and couldn't be a part of raising her), only to later see the universe had a plan after all.

A year after making that decision, I met my husband, and together, we've worked to break cycles and raise our child with healthy attachment, safety, boundaries, and so much love. Breaking multiple cycles of trauma in how we've raised her has healed so many parts of me and truly has been one of my life's greatest feats.

I've had to detach from and cut contact with certain family members, accepting with a heavy heart that I cannot change others. I no longer have to accept unacceptable behavior. I can practice love, compassion, and acceptance from a safe distance. I've watched old patterns play out in work relationships and had the courage to know when to move on. I've experienced beautiful moments of repair in relationships, like the one with my mother, and we've healed together. I have formed real friendships, traveled to amazing places in the world, and discovered how much I love to travel—how my soul craves to experience.

Recovery has allowed me to do things truly beyond my wildest dreams— obtain my Master's degree in Clinical Social Work from a prestigious university in Manhattan, graduate with the highest honors, attain dual licensure, train to specialize in the treatment of addiction and trauma, and complete a trauma-informed yoga certification. During my time as director, I developed the programming and clinical team for a local addiction treatment center. I've since become a business owner of a private therapy practice with my two partners, whom I adore and continue to learn and grow from. Each day, I find purpose in helping other people find their path to healing. I've built a beautiful family with my daughter and husband. Our home is full of love. I've made amends for my past and contributed back to society in meaningful ways. The list of blessings goes on, and I'm grateful for each one.

The accomplishments, the milestones, the visible markers of change— these are the external things that people see when they look at me now. The invisible things are far more valuable. There have been moments of awe that ripple through me--- like standing on the edge of a cliff with my husband in Saint Croix, smelling the salt breeze, or whipping down a ski slope with my daughter and brother beside me; climbing a Banyan tree nestling in its arms like a real-life fairy; watching the sunrise from Rialto Bridge with my best friend in Venice. And there are the quieter moments—snuggling with my child or my pug, suppressing a giggle at how they both snore. Pulling into the driveway of my home and knowing what 'home' actually feels like. Dragging my body out of bed and doing yoga in the grass, feeling myself wake up to a new day. Taking a breath and finally feeling grateful and worthy to be here in this life.

I wake up without wanting to die anymore. The waves of self-hatred that consumed me have quieted, leaving a sense of calm in my inner world. I no longer feel the need to escape because I've built a life, I actually wish to be present in.

I used to see myself as a living dead girl, broken, empty, and a black hole of a human being. Today I know better. Even on my worst days, I am alive, I am full of light, and I am full of hope and possibility. Many years ago, I was introduced to the Japanese pottery "kintsugi", where the cracks of broken pottery are filled with gold or other precious metal—the idea being that rather than "fix" or hide those cracks, we should find appreciation and reverence for their beauty. No matter how broken, damaged, or alone you might think you are, my path has truly shown me that 'where there is breath there is hope'. Whatever painful beliefs you've been holding down deep, you don't have to stay tied to them in the darkness of secrecy—freedom is possible. The strength and beauty of who we are reside in the fractured parts of ourselves and in our individual stories. It starts with simply inviting in the possibility of "maybe me" and taking those first shaky steps on the path to healing. You don't have to overcome or heal it all at once; just start by believing that what has been possible for me can be possible for you too.

Lisa Cordasco, MSW, LCSW, LCADC, CCS, CCTP, C-DBT, RYT-200

Lisa Cordasco has over a decade of experience in the behavioral health field and is one of the co-founders of *Rewired Path Counseling and Consultation*. She entered the field after finding a calling to help others heal, having built a foundation in her own recovery.

Lisa holds licensure as a clinical social worker and clinical alcohol and drug counselor, earned through her Master's degree at Fordham University. Lisa has gone on to pursue further training and specializations in complex trauma, grief, and the mind-body connection. Known for her deeply compassionate yet firm approach, Lisa integrates a dialectical view in her work.

Outside of her professional life, Lisa enjoys nature, yoga, and creative expression. She loves traveling the world with her daughter, spouse, pet pug, and found family. Her favorite time of day is sunrise, and she's been known to wake up everyone traveling with her to watch the new day make its entrance. Lisa believes in holding reverence for the preciousness of life in the little moments.

www.rewiredpath.com
lcordasco@rewiredpath.com

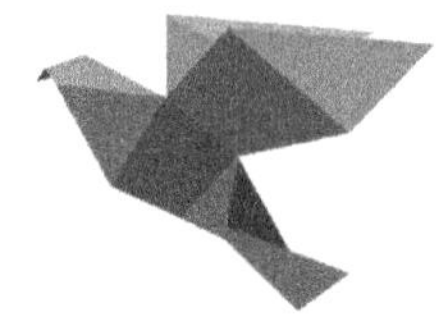

CHAPTER 7

Forged in the Crucible of Absurdity: Finding the Light in Life's Darkest Corners

Justin MacDonald, LCPC, LPC, NCC, MHRT/C

My earliest memory is one of chaos and confusion. I was five years old, sitting on the couch, crying as my mom changed the locks on our front door. She was telling my dad he couldn't live here anymore, and at that moment, my five-year-old world was falling apart. At the time, I couldn't understand the complexity of the situation—only that my parents were separating, and it felt like my family was breaking beyond repair.

As a child, that memory was clear and sharp, but as I grew older, I came to understand the layers behind it. My dad was desperate to keep our family together, and my mom, who needed a break for her mental health, had reached her limit. This memory is the one I hold on to most from my childhood, and while it's muddled with emotions, it marked a pivotal moment in my life. My siblings, Kai and Heather, both struggle with identity, reality experiencing, mental health situations, and substance abuse issues. At various points, one, the other, or both were confidants and supports when I needed them.

My dad became what I can only describe as the human embodiment of Eeyore—constantly sad and heavy-hearted. He loved Eeyore, and in many ways, he became a personification of grief. My mom, on the other hand, faced her own mental health challenges, but always rooted for me, no matter how difficult I made things for her. She was there for me through everything, even as I gave her hell during those early years. There were many points in my years using drugs where I forced my mother into withdrawal as I placed my need for drugs above hers. She had significant back pain and was linked up with a pain management doctor who has since lost their license to practice. Imagine being so "selfed up" that you forced someone into extreme pain so that you wouldn't have to face a relatively cushy reality. This culminated with my mother kicking me out and telling my dad that he had to deal with me and get me back in line because she couldn't put up with my behavior and nastiness.

Their separation coincided with what felt like my own internal unraveling. Whether it was a result of their split or my ADHD diagnosis, things spiraled out of control for me.

School consisted of my starting fights with kids smaller than me, my size, and kids larger than me. I couldn't keep my mouth shut and didn't have a filter, so I interrupted everyone and told them what I thought of them. Starting in elementary school, my lack of filter and verbal impulsivity had me telling kids twice my size to "take your busted ass face and go eat some dog food," which would routinely lead to me getting into fights. Later in life, this transitioned to me identifying people's emotional trigger points and either intentionally or unintentionally activating those hurt points. One exchange went as follows: Person A shared how they didn't have any real place to live besides their parents' house or any real income. Going on to say how they started moving more and more stuff into this partner's expensive apartment and using money they got from them to purchase groceries to put into their own bank account, then intentionally purchase less food than the amount of money provided to them so that they could have money in their account. They went on to describe how they make statements along the lines of "things are just getting so expensive" after purchasing that food, not with the money their partner provided, but with their own credit card. I replied, "So you're telling me that you are a great manipulator and liar?" I then chuckled heartily before realizing they probably didn't land well, regardless of there being truth and honesty in them. In second grade, the school principal issued my mother an ultimatum: "Justin cannot come back to school until he is medicated." That was the start of what would be a long and challenging relationship with medication. At just seven years old, I began a journey with dependency that would eventually lead to addiction. It didn't take long for me to figure out how to misuse the ADHD medication I was given. By fifth grade, I was smoking cigarettes, smoking weed, drinking, stealing my mom's pills, and snorting heroin. I was a small kid, barely 10 or 11, but using substances made me feel less—a lot less of everything. It numbed the chaos inside me and gave me an escape from the confusion of my emotions.

As someone with ADHD, I will hear 20,000 more negative statements directed at me than people without ADHD. This, in and of itself, sets the stage for a sense of "othering" that is insidious, especially when coupled with the understanding of othering that is a baseline for most people who use drugs in maladaptive ways. Until I discovered the above statistic, I could not put my finger on, nor had the words to describe, why I never felt accepted, appreciated, valued, or loved as other kids and people spoke about feeling. This presented as a kind of cognitive dissonance that was somewhat unidentifiable until it was too far into my life.

As I got older, my behavior became more destructive. It wasn't long before I found myself in situations I couldn't control. I was running from cops, getting arrested, and eventually ended up in a deflection and diversion program in D.C. called "Time Dollar Court." This program was helpful in many ways and taxing in other ways. Time Dollar Court consisted of weekend classes on math, time management, role-plays, and "being a good citizen" rhetoric. At the end of those classes, I sat in front of youth close to my own age who had previously graduated from this program, and they asked me questions about what I'd learned and how it would impact my choices moving forward. They then decided, with input from Time Dollar Court-employed adults, whether my responsibilities and work in the classes constituted my graduating from the program and whether I had learned anything of positive impact that would influence my future decisions. The summer I attended the program, my father had accepted a new position with his current employer at a location in another state, a couple of hours away. Every Saturday morning, while I was going to the education classes, we had to wake up at 4 a.m. to drive across Maryland to get to D.C. in time for me to attend Time Dollar Court, so I didn't get sent to jail.

At home, things weren't much better. I started using drugs with family members and even stealing my mom's pain meds, which forced her into withdrawal. I was on probation, and one particularly bad night ended with me having my stomach pumped and a catheter inserted. I was barely a teenager, but I felt like my life was already out of control.

My earliest romantic relationship was unhealthy. I was fifteen, and he was twenty-five, and it was mainly a way to get drugs. And while we used each other, things for things, I only understood later that I was a victim. Another memory I keep stored away. Looking back now, I'm dumbfounded that I didn't end up in an even worse situation.

Just before I turned eighteen, something shifted. I was on probation at the time, and through a combination of luck, the support of my girlfriend, and my need to prove people wrong or right, I managed to get clean. She was one of the impetuses for my life change. While that relationship had its own unhealthy elements of codependency, I am still grateful to her for steering me toward recovery. Her presence in my life at that time may have saved me.

The other impetus for me getting clean was something a drug and alcohol counselor said during the intensive outpatient program my probation officer sent me to. I was there for not being able to pee when it was time to pee, knowing I was going to pop positive. That counselor's name was Gwen. On the first night, she said, "One out of the thirty of you is gonna get clean, stay clean, and do things differently. Those are not good odds." It was a strange mix of wanting to show up for someone else and a deep-seated sense of "I'll show you!" I have often said, "I got clean out of spite", but looking back, it seems more like I got clean out of a deep-seated need to be accepted and loved.

Just after celebrating my first year of recovery in Salisbury, MD, I found myself attending orientation at UArts in Philly. This was after not knowing whether or not I was going to graduate high school due to the wreckage of my drug use. It was early during my time in Philly when I met an amazingly impactful mentor in my life, even to this day, Victor. Victor carried himself in a way that I respected and appreciated. He lived the "Diana Ross" story with all the love, shade, and humor to boot. He was a no-nonsense person who could find light in the darkest corners of his world. To this day, his integrity, joviality, and mischievousness are always something to strive for.

During my early recovery, I turned to books to help me process everything I had been through. I found solace in Viktor Frankl's *Man's Search for Meaning*, and his perspective about finding purpose in suffering resonated deeply with me. He described resilience in his own words, before the term had even entered the psychological lexicon. His ideas mirrored the existentialist philosophy that I would later adopt, the belief that suffering could be a path to meaning. Frankl's thoughts aligned with

Nietzsche's famous quote: "He who has a why to live can bear almost any how." That idea became a foundation for how I saw the world.

I also read Haruki Murakami's surreal stories, which offered me an escape from reality while simultaneously making me confront it. Poetry by Nâzım Hikmet spoke to my emotions in ways that nothing else could. Additionally, I encountered the work of philosopher Jerome Miller, whose book *In the Throe of Wonder* became a significant influence on my worldview. These works, taken together, shaped my philosophy of life, which I call Absurd Existentialism. It's the belief that life itself has no inherent meaning, but that we, as individuals, are responsible for creating our own purpose. This philosophy gave me a framework for understanding my own suffering and the chaos that had defined my life up until that point.

"I'm resilient, aren't I? I'm not dead yet … really … I'm sixteen years past my expiration date." Before getting clean, I couldn't imagine a future for myself. I didn't think I'd live past twenty-one, and certainly never envisioned becoming a mentor, father, husband, or ex-husband. I couldn't fathom a life where I'd be sharing my story with others, offering them a glimpse into my experience with addiction and recovery. And yet, here I am—sixteen years beyond the expiration date I had mentally set for myself. When I reflect on that, I realize just how resilient I am. I've survived more than I ever thought I could, and while life has often felt absurd, I have found meaning in the most unlikely of places.

From the concept of resilience, I developed what I call brutal positivity. This idea is rooted in the lessons I learned from the D.C. punk scene, which was just as influential to me as Frankl or Murakami. When I moved to D.C., I started getting into punk music. I started listening to bands like *The Profit$*, *Crass*, *Iskra*, *Disease Called Man*, *Capitalist Casualties*, and *Antischism*. At first, I was drawn to the scene and the lifestyle. I liked the raw energy of the music, the way it seemed to scream everything I was feeling inside. But as I got older, I began to appreciate the deeper themes of punk. The lyrics often dealt with personal struggles, mental health, a sense of alienation from society, a deep connection to various subcultures, and subversive thoughts. These were feelings I relate to all too well.

On the surface, punk music might seem like it's full of angst and anger, but at its core, it promotes community, activism, and optimism through rebellion. Punk taught me that it's okay to be angry at the world, but that anger doesn't have to be destructive; it can be a force for positive change. That's where brutal positivity grew from resilience. It is facing the brutality of life head-on and refusing to let it extinguish your inner spark. It's about maintaining hope, even when everything around you feels hopeless.

As I continued my recovery, Victor, my confidant and mentor, was a tremendous help. Victor was diagnosed with ALS and watching him disappear in the grips of such a condition was painstaking. He walked me through the steps, even when he couldn't walk. He was a character, larger than life in most moments, lighting up every room he entered, even if shade was being thrown his way. His mind was as sharp as a tack, but his muscles just were not doing what they needed to do. A sponsee brother called, telling me to see him immediately. He died shortly after I was able to make eye contact with him. His vibrance still shines in my eyes. His death seemed to have begun a windfall of grief.

After his death, I moved forward with resilience and proceeded with my academic career. However, two years into what should have been a three-year master's program, life took another unexpected turn. My mom was diagnosed with stage four lung cancer. She likely had less than a year to live, and she needed to get her things in order. My parents had moved back in together years prior, so they could both be near their first grandchild in Philadelphia. However, my mom didn't want to live with her ex-husband. So, my sister, Heather, put up the money for a place in Fishtown since Kai and I didn't have the extra money.

Just two weeks later, Heather found my father dead. We think my mom had been keeping him alive all those years. He would take his insulin and forget to eat, which would make his blood sugar dangerously low, and he would get belligerent. He had been forgetting things more frequently but did not seek any neurological testing. My father likely died because he took his insulin and forgot to eat—but this time, there was no one there to call 911. He died alone, probably scared, and unaware of what was happening. I do not want his story to be mine.

I tried to finish out that semester strong, but I couldn't. I ended up taking several semesters off to help care for my mother, along with my siblings, during her last days. I spent that time giving my mother Tylenol three suppositories during her final days for palliative care. I was at a recovery meeting when Kai called, saying, "You need to get back here, Justin; she won't be here much longer." I biked through every red light on the way home, ironically almost dying, hoping to steal one more of her breaths while at her side.

She died before I made it back home.

If you ever meet me, ask me about the tattoo I have on my right index finger. After my mother's death, I wanted a token of remembrance. I thought about the resilience it took to step away from school for several semesters to care for her and instinctively knew I wanted something permanent to mark that chapter. That led me to a simple line tattoo below the first crease of my digit. To some, it might seem insignificant, but that finger holds deep meaning; it's the same one I used to give her medication, a small yet profound reminder of how present I was for her. It is a sadly comical tattoo that reminds me of the universe's tragic humor. As I processed her death, my recovery was the only thing that kept me alive after she died.

Life continued to take unexpected turns, with grief piling on in ways I could not anticipate. My parents' death sent Heather into a deeper use of drugs, and in 2022, she passed away. Less than a year before she suspiciously died, she had been diagnosed as having bipolar disorder. She favored opiates and benzodiazepines over the coke or crack that was concluded to have resulted in her overdose. The circumstances surrounding her death felt suspicious to me, but the cops didn't think there was anything suspicious about a "junkie" OD'ing.

I sat with her while she was unresponsive and in a vegetative state. Even after they removed the life support, she continued breathing for too long to remain viable to be donated to science. It felt like a final act of defiance, a refusal to conform to expectations. Heather always liked things on her own terms or not at all. While I can appreciate that approach, I continue to strive to navigate life with resilience and flexibility, ensuring I don't endanger myself or others.

Their absence in my life is the most strenuous part of forging forward. I wanted them all to be a physical part of my family's story. I wanted them to meet my children and those I care about whom I meet along the way. The antifragility here is my appreciation of everything that I have. The writing of this only deepens my gratitude. My grief for their absence only solidifies my desire to be present for as long as possible in the lives of those I care about. Those close to me will only know them through the stories they hear of them. They will only see them in my actions.

Today, my life is vastly different from what it was during my teenage years. Instead of running from cops, I began working alongside them. I served as a community mental health liaison for two rural county sheriff's departments. I connected the people in these communities with resources that the police couldn't, and understandably, shouldn't provide. The work I did was difficult and draining, but it was also incredibly fulfilling. I saw firsthand the struggles people faced, from systemic failures to the grief that comes with losing someone to suicide. My role required a balance of optimism and realism, and I did and continue to do my best to bring both to the table in every interaction I have.

In addition to my work with law enforcement, I also moonlight as a private therapist, providing individual, couples, and family therapy. It's a continuation of the work I do in my day job, but on a more personal level. I'm constantly reminded of how important it is to maintain a sense of positivity, even in the face of overwhelming challenges. The communities I serve are often dealing with problems far beyond their control, and it's my job to help them navigate those difficulties as best I can. While my work is emotionally draining, constantly emptying my cup, it gets refilled regularly because it is gratifying and meaningful. I wouldn't trade it for anything.

As mentioned earlier, I was diagnosed with ADHD at a young age, and while it has posed challenges, I've come to see it as one of my greatest assets. My neurodivergence allows me to adapt quickly in times of crisis, and it's been a key factor in my ability to cultivate antifragility in my life.

Antifragility is a concept presented by Nassim Taleb. It goes beyond resilience. While resilience is about bouncing back to baseline after adversity, antifragility is about growing stronger and more robust because of it. I've faced many challenges in my life, both personal and systemic, but each one has strengthened me in some way.

Of course, that doesn't mean the journey has been easy. I still struggle with impulse control, especially when it comes to my relationship with money and food. There are areas of my life that require constant work.

But I approach these challenges with the mindset that growth is a lifelong process. I believe that there is always room for improvement, and I try to embrace that philosophy in everything I do.

When my ex-wife told me, "You are so intensely human," I felt seen in a way that I hadn't before. It is one of the greatest compliments I've ever received, because it acknowledged both my strengths and flaws. I am an intensely human absurd existentialist, driven by a brutal positivity that refuses to be extinguished by life's absurdities and nature's chaos. I never thought I would work with law enforcement to make amends for the harm I caused as a kid. I never thought I'd be a husband, an ex-husband, or a father. And yet, here I am, living a life that is far beyond anything I could have imagined when I was younger.

Looking back, I realize that I have been following the path of antifragility my whole life. Every hardship, every challenge, every moment of chaos has strengthened me. My recovery is ongoing, and while I know I will face more challenges in the future, I also know that I will grow from those experiences, just as I have grown from everything I've faced.

A good friend of mine likes to tell people (me especially): "Do better." It's not a command or a judgment, but a reminder that we all have the capacity for growth, no matter where we are in life.

I've spent years navigating trauma, addiction, and mental health struggles, but I've come out on the other side with a deeper understanding of myself and the world around me. I'm grateful to the people who have supported me along the way - my family, friends, mentors, and the people I serve in my community. Together, we've shared moments of pain, joy, and hope, and those connections have been a vital part of my journey toward antifragility through resilience and brutal positivity.

Absurd existentialism holds that nothing in this universe makes sense, except what we decide does. In line with this and my take on Viktor Frankl's core thought in *Man's Search for Meaning*, we suffer to meaning: pain is unavoidable; suffering might be avoidable, but for me it sets the context for suffering opposite: growth. I cannot have one without the other. I must appreciate how I suffer and struggle, and learn to appreciate better, and even influence how I grow and prosper because of it. This is all wrapped up in my idea of brutal positivity. It starts with absurdism, folds in suffering to meaning, taps into antifragility, touches on the Buddhist separation of pain and suffering, and amounts to the following for the reader, if you so choose to accept: From the complex parts of your life, how have you leveraged those to be a better person? How have you leaned so far into the sticking points of your life to use those points as pivots and trajectory-changing or elevating points to be better than before? Have you done this? I bet you have. Whether you spend time seeing and acknowledging that is another question entirely.

And so, I continue forward, one day at a time, always striving to do better. I am Justin Ritchie MacDonald: a resilient, brutally positive, anti-fragile, intensely human absurd existentialist. As I see it, there is no other way to be: human.

Justin MacDonald, LCPC, LPC, NCC, MHRT/C

I am a person living with long-term recovery both from substance use issues and mental health challenges. My passion has always been to help people and create a positive impact on the world. An opportunity came my way that led me to a wonderful place, working in diversion and deflection away from law enforcement and the justice system in rural Maine, focusing on crisis mitigation, people with mental health difficulties, those with substance use issues, and folks in need of connecting with resources. I am now back in the Philly area, working remotely, supporting individuals with OCD, anxiety, specific phobias, and depression.

I also provide individual, family, and couples therapy via telehealth to residents of Maine and Pennsylvania. I strive to create a space where people feel comfortable discussing complex topics, provide easily implementable coping skills and strategies, find strength-based short- and long-term solutions, and help clients identify and create meaning and purpose in their lives.

CHAPTER 8

An Angel in Motion: From Survival to Service
Susan Long, MSW, LSW, LCADC

I'll never forget the night the SWAT team kicked in the doors of the unstable, dangerous house where I was living deep in my addiction. Officers pointed guns at us as they swarmed inside. I sat up so fast my heart nearly exploded out of my chest. As they dragged people out in handcuffs, one officer, who I used to serve as a bartender, looked at me, baffled. "Susie ... what are you doing?" he asked. The truth was, going to jail wasn't my main concern. All I could think about was not getting sick and how I was going to get more pills. That was the sad reality of where addiction had taken me. But my story didn't begin there.

Growing up in Pennsauken, New Jersey, left me with many fond memories that still warm my heart today. I had many great childhood pals, but my best friends were Amber and Tommy. Summers brimmed with chasing lightning bugs, playing in the leaf compost by the creek, and strolling to Mister Softee to get my favorite treat: a twinkle-top ice cream cone. Amber and I would talk on the house phone, agreeing to meet halfway between our houses—no cell phones, computers, or distractions. Life felt so simple then. Amber and I dreamed of growing old together, sitting around playing spades and knitting. One day, we would get a big van, search the streets, and rescue homeless animals.

But simplicity was fleeting, as childhood innocence gave way to struggles that shaped the course of my life. My parents divorced when I was in elementary school. Looking back, I'm grateful they parted ways when I was still young, because our house was often like a war zone. My father has been fighting his own demons his entire life, but he did the best he could for me. I knew he loved me endlessly. Despite working long hours, my mom provided constant care for my brother and me, making sure we had dinner together every night. I'll always remember her leaving balloons by my bed on Valentine's Day. Unfortunately, my parents' love wasn't enough to shield me from the trouble ahead.

Severe social anxiety and ADHD, combined with childhood trauma and a genetic predisposition to substance use disorder, led me down a tumultuous path. My mom encouraged me to join Girl Scouts and play sports, but I didn't know anyone there. Despite genuinely wanting to make friends, I remained paralyzed with fear, silent and invisible. Middle school terrified me: suddenly, I wasn't just with the neighborhood kids. By age twelve, I was already using substances, along with lying and shoplifting, desperate to feel accepted, normal, and funny. Alcohol and drugs made me feel all those things—until they didn't.

I'll never forget the first time I got drunk. It was a Wednesday night in seventh grade. Perfect timing, as my mom was out for the night at her bowling league. My friend Kim and I made fuzzy navels with the peach schnapps I nabbed from our kitchen cabinet. With our cocktails, we smoked Kent cigarettes stolen from my stepfather. As I walked Kim home that night, I dropped my drink, spilling it all over the sidewalk. I got on my knees and drank from the cement with a straw. This struck me as hilarious at the time, but in retrospect, I see it was a glaring indicator of problems to come.

High school marked the beginning of deeper struggles, during which I frequently clashed with authority figures. While a few kindhearted teachers made me feel valued, most were quick to judge me as a "bad kid." At the time, I felt misunderstood, though in hindsight, I see how my actions fueled those judgments—I was selling drugs out of my locker and was escorted out of prom by undercover cops. These dysfunctional habits spilled over into my social life, where one unhealthy relationship led to another. Since age twelve, I lied, cheated, and cycled through boyfriends, alternating between victim and abuser. Eventually, in a desperate bid for a normal life, I married my first husband, Joe, who was a police officer, imagining myself becoming a "Susie homemaker." I dreamed of having it all together—the beautiful house with a white picket fence and the feeling of finally being "normal." I wanted it so badly, I tried to believe it was possible. But the truth was, I wasn't capable. I walked down the aisle with blurry eyes, convincing myself love and marriage would be enough to heal what was broken inside me. I was not capable of a healthy, loving relationship with anyone, including myself. My chaos followed me, and that first marriage quickly crumbled under the weight of the issues I hadn't yet faced.

The majority of my former life feels like a blur, clouded by years of self-medicating with drugs, alcohol, and bad decisions. I was trapped in codependency, frantically searching for love, but without any model for a healthy relationship, self-love, or respect, my efforts were doomed from the start. The loneliness I felt pushed me further into isolation, leading me to retreat from my life and squander my potential. I became the picture of "wasted talent," my life a scene from *Groundhog Day*—repetitive, meaningless, and empty.

My grandmother—Mom Mom—didn't drive, so I would make the trip down to Ocean City to take her food shopping or to her appointments. Sometimes we'd grab Chinese food, and back at her house, she'd make me the best grilled cheese sandwiches with Cracker Barrel Vermont sharp cheese. She always kept a candy jar overflowing with Hershey's

Kisses and other sweets, as if she never wanted anyone to leave without a little treat. She had a way of making even the simplest moments feel special. Whenever I was with her, she'd smile and say, "Anything your little heart desires." With her, I felt comfort and safety; I struggled to find anywhere else. Losing my beloved grandmother was the final crack in the fragile foundation of my life. Already numb, I spiraled deeper into gambling, cocaine, alcohol, pills — anything that could temporarily dull the pain I couldn't escape.

During the breakdown of my marriage, I left Joe for a man I had worked with as a bartender. Bill and I tried to build a life together, but it revolved around drugs, fighting, and crime rather than love or stability. As mentioned earlier, the SWAT team, the prosecutor's office, and local police kicked in our apartment door. I woke with sirens in my ears and guns in my face. Facing charges, Bill went on the run across the country. Somehow, I escaped legal consequences, but I felt the urge to start running too—away from my life, my family, and Joe. I followed Bill west, unaware that I was beginning a journey to hell.

Living in the 120-degree Las Vegas summer, addicted to crystal meth, I was 83 pounds, homeless, and trapped in an abusive relationship. I spent my days getting high, panhandling, eating out of dumpsters, walking up and down Boulder Highway, and hiding in casinos, gambling to escape reality. I believed my loved ones would be better off without me, though it crushes me to imagine how my parents must have felt, wondering if I was living or dead. I thought I could outrun my problems, but as they say, "Wherever you go, there you are." Weeks without sleep left me battered, bruised, and broken, both inside and out. Lying under vending machines, Coinstar machines, and laundromat dryers, I hoped in vain to find change.

One especially bleak day, the sun was so relentless it felt like it had to be 130 degrees. My feet were hard, dry, and black from walking the streets, each step aching against the burning pavement. My body felt hollow, weak, and starved, and I had never felt so thirsty or malnourished in my entire life. My tongue stuck to the roof of my mouth, and every breath carried the weight of heat and hopelessness. Certain I might collapse right there from thirst and despair, I stumbled toward a church in a last-ditch attempt to find solace, maybe even mercy. But when I pushed open the door, all I found was emptiness. I slid my hands down the locked doors and stumbled towards a 7-Eleven, begging for a cup to fill with water. The clerk refused but said I could drink straight from the faucet instead. I will never, ever forget how it felt to be treated that way, as if I were less than human. But I'll also always remember how it felt to have a stranger tell me to grab the biggest cup, fill it with whatever I wanted, and meet her at the cash register. With kindness, she told me, "I've been there before."

I was too delusional to grasp what she meant: that life could be different, that recovery was possible. I was trapped, scared to keep living this way, but equally terrified to die. I didn't know how to exist with or without drugs. The idea of making it out of Vegas alive felt impossible. Every day, thoughts of walking into traffic to end my misery consumed me.

Out there, in the middle of all the darkness, I had a friend named Tyrone who always tried to look out for me. Before he went to jail, he told Bill to get me a cat. I think Tyrone was afraid for me, and he knew how easily people could take advantage of me when I was vulnerable. Not long after, someone handed me a book bag, and inside was a beautiful black-and-white kitten with huge eyes and ears too big for her tiny face. I pulled her out, and she blinked up at me like she was just as uncertain about me as I was about life.

I named her Miss Thomas, and she became the only light in my life at that time. In a world where everything felt unstable, she gave me something pure to hold on to. Caring for her gave me a reason to keep going; she needed me as much as I needed her. I couldn't always take care of her the way she deserved—most days I could barely take care of myself — but I loved her more than I loved myself. In a strange way, that little kitten and I saved each other. She reminded me that, somewhere inside all the chaos and self-destruction, I was still capable of love.

Meanwhile, Bill and I were so mired in the chaos of addiction and dysfunction that we couldn't take care of ourselves, let alone each other. Deep down, I knew if I stayed, I wouldn't survive. We were constantly on the verge of literally killing each other. Whether through murder, overdose, or suicide, something would inevitably take me out for good. As the days blurred into each other, desperation finally overcame me, and I reached out to Joe for support. In November 2013, he flew across the country, hung up missing person signs, and found me. I will never forget sitting at a slot machine at Sam's Town casino with my Phillies hat on, playing one penny at a time, and I looked up, and there he was. Joe's unwavering support reminded me I wasn't as alone as I believed. It planted the first seed of hope that I might still have a future. He saved my life.

Together, we flew home, and my best friend from Pennsauken, Tommy, let me stay with him. I could hardly stand or speak in complete sentences. My ID and most of my possessions had been lost in Vegas—my mind and teeth included. I couldn't even get a library card. I was wallowing in self-pity, terrified of my surroundings. Vulnerability overwhelmed me; I felt like I was standing naked in Times Square on New Year's Eve. Without drugs, I was once again that quiet little girl, filled with fear and self-doubt. I hid inside for a long time, afraid to face the outside world.

Joe dropped off a list of twelve-step meetings at Tommy's house. My mom would drive me, or I'd take the bus. I was still petrified of interacting with others—sometimes I would walk past the meeting place—but eventually I found the courage I needed. My first meeting was in a cold basement in Ventnor, where people shared their stories with smiles and gratitude. At first, their cheerful spirits in that chilly room confused me, but now it makes perfect sense. An old-timer, Johnny A, told me to come back, and that is what I did. I believed what I read in the literature and knew there was a solution. In those early years, I walked into meetings with my head down, too ashamed to look anyone in the eye.

Despite my initial resolve to stay sober, the crushing weight of my anxiety pushed me back toward old habits. Less than two months later, I relapsed, drinking alcohol, gambling, and using cocaine at The Showboat in Atlantic City. As my supply dwindled, I felt increasingly desperate. Memories of Las Vegas haunted me—the relentless pain, the crushing desperation, and the downward spiral that had become my life. The very thought of reliving that torment filled me with dread, and I knew I couldn't let history repeat itself.

I had an epiphany: I could go back to the pain and shame of my past, or I could accept the love, guidance, and support of others like me in that basement meeting. The next day, I chose to surrender to recovery. I went to a speaker meeting and found my first sponsor. That moment marked a turning point in my life. From then on, no matter how intense the challenges or how overwhelming life has felt, I've never picked up another drink or drug. The fear of returning to that dark place fuels my determination to keep moving forward.

Through prayer, group trauma therapy, outpatient treatment, and working the steps, I began to understand that forgiveness wasn't just about letting others off the hook—it was about freeing myself from the burdens of guilt, shame, and resentment. Learning to love and forgive myself was the first step toward truly believing I was worthy of a better life. As my trust in God deepened and I found the courage to make amends with those I had hurt, I discovered that forgiveness was a powerful tool for healing old wounds. It allowed me to move forward without carrying the weight of the past.

During this time, I came to appreciate the transformative value of honesty, perseverance, adaptability, and integrity. These principles became a guiding light in my recovery. I realized I had to care for my body and mind with the same devotion I brought to my spiritual practices. I found genuine peace and discovered that a life shaped by self-forgiveness, accountability, and compassion was not only possible but deeply rewarding. After about seven years of sobriety, I could finally hold my head up confidently and look others in their eyes. Through surrender and commitment to recovery, I began to rebuild my life.

Seeking help and stability, I became a client of the Atlantic Homeless Alliance at social services in Atlantic City. Two compassionate social workers treated me with dignity, empathy, and respect, genuinely wanting to help. Their support inspired me to become a social worker, and I promised them I'd make it happen one day. Motivated to make up for years of lost purpose and self-worth, I took classes at ACCC and Rutgers University, earning my bachelor's degree in 2017 and my Master's in 2018. Today, I'm deeply proud of my service-based career as a licensed social worker and alcohol and drug counselor. At one point, I worked as a supervisor at the Atlantic Homeless Alliance—the very place where I'd first received help—a true full-circle moment. It took a long time to believe that all these beautiful changes were happening, and even longer for my outer life to finally align with my inner growth.

While my recovery brought many blessings, it also brought unexpected heartache, like losing Amber in 2015, before she had the chance to see me sober. My heart still aches from her loss, but her letters, filled with pride in my recovery journey, remind me she's one of my guardian angels. In her memory, I plan to create a healing place for animals and humans, calling it The Blue Nest, after her middle name. Every morning, when I see blue jays and cardinals in my yard, I feel her presence, inspiring me to fulfill the wonderful dreams we once shared.

Gardening and practicing yoga have become passions of mine. With a scattered mind full of big ideas, I often forget to breathe. Yoga brings me back to my breath. Consistent practice has helped me heal from past trauma and manage everyday stress. There's a special place in Atlantic City called The Leadership Studio. It's one of the first nonprofit yoga studios in the country, dedicated to making yoga accessible to everyone, regardless of their ability to pay. Upon my first step through the door, I felt at home, loved, and never judged. Inspired by my experience, I wrote this poem:

Healing at The Leadership Studio

Water, sounds of the waves
Smell of the salt
Echoes from gulls
Safe space at leadership
Hot, calm, yet moving fast
Freeing to my mind and spirit
Nurturing to my soul
The flow of the breath cooling my nose
and calming the chaos in my head

In my early recovery, I fell in love twice: once with the organization Angels in Motion and once with my husband, David. David and I used to see each other on the 505 NJ Transit bus: me going to IOP, and him heading to his job or recovery court. After talking at a 12-step meeting, we met for a fateful lunch at Applebee's the next day—and the rest is history! For the first time in my life, I can say that I'm faithful and devoted to him and our love. This December, we'll celebrate our sixth wedding anniversary. We have a beautiful little home in Northfield, New Jersey, filled with love, cats, and of course, Miss Thomas.

While my relationship with David brought me joy and stability, I found a renewed sense of purpose in a place I never expected. In 2015, I learned about an opportunity to volunteer in Kensington through a street outreach organization called Angels in Motion. The compassion and kindness that Angels in Motion showed to those struggling on the streets and within the community moved me to tears. Instead of looking away from people like me, they sat with them and listened. Instead of disdain or pity, they offered blessing bags, resources, and hugs. I dove in headfirst and knew I had to be a part of it.

Inspired, I began handing out blessing bags in Camden while attending Rutgers University, eventually founding the New Jersey Chapter of Angels in Motion in 2017. The organization continues to grow through the dedication of selfless volunteers and the community's generosity. We've recently opened a community wellness center, offering compassionate support for individuals struggling with substance use disorders, mental health challenges, and homelessness. Seeing those we once helped now thriving in recovery and volunteering alongside us is profoundly rewarding. This shared commitment and community have helped heal my once-fractured foundation. My true passion lies not in boardrooms or offices, but in directly connecting with those in need in alleys and on the streets, where I feel most purposeful and fulfilled.

Angels in Motion gave my life meaning, and for that I'll always be grateful. I've learned to never give up on anyone, including myself. People can change every day. I truly believe that the most important ingredient in helping others is meeting them where they are—physically, mentally, and emotionally. It's letting them know you believe in them and that they, too, have a purpose. Recovery introduced me to wonderful people, and I've had the honor of helping the most generous, loving souls. The folks I meet living on the streets would gladly give me the shirt off their back or share their last meal with me.

These experiences have left a lasting impact, inspiring me to approach this beautiful world with curiosity and a deep desire for connection. I still struggle with social anxiety, but I've realized that people aren't as intimidating as I once believed. Many of us wrestle with our own self-doubt, and ultimately, we all share a common desire: to be accepted and loved. Embracing vulnerability and openness is essential to fostering genuine human connection and community, as I know firsthand.

I'm incredibly proud of the person I've become and the life I lead. As Shakespeare said, "To thine own self be true." Through recovery, I've learned to embrace vulnerability, authenticity, and the power of connection. Each step of this journey, from the depths of despair to rediscovering my purpose, has taught me that transformation is possible when we meet others—and ourselves—with love, compassion, and empathy. I no longer need substances to survive, and every morning I wake up with immense gratitude for this second chance. While I carry the weight of those I've lost to addiction, I honor their memory by living purposefully and serving others. The freedom I feel today is a gift I never thought I'd receive; it fuels my commitment to help others find their own path to healing and a life filled with hope and meaning.

If you're in the place I once was, please know that help is available and that you are worthy of a healthy, happy life. I thought my life was over, that I had no worth outside of chasing the next high or numbing the next withdrawal. But recovery showed me otherwise. It wasn't a piece of cake. I've stumbled, I've had immense loss, I've struggled, and I've had to rebuild piece by piece.

Today I can tell you that change is possible. If you feel hopeless, reach out for help. Ask for it before it feels too late. Hold on to the smallest reason — a pet, a friend, a dream — because sometimes that little reason is enough to keep you alive until you can find a bigger one. You are stronger than you realize, and healing is waiting for you, just as it was for me.

Susan Long, MSW, LSW, LCADC

Susan Long leads Angels in Motion as its Executive Director, blending professional training with a heart for service. A licensed social worker and alcohol and drug counselor, she earned her social work degree at Rutgers University. Beyond her role at AIM, Susan volunteers at Adelaide's Place in Atlantic City, supporting women facing homelessness.

Her work is grounded in compassion, resilience, and the belief that small acts of kindness ripple into lasting change. At home in Northfield, New Jersey, Susan enjoys yoga, gardening, and time with her husband David and their beloved cats.

www.aimangelsinmotion.org

email:Susanlong@njangelsinmotion.org

facebook.com/AIM.AngelsInMotionNJ

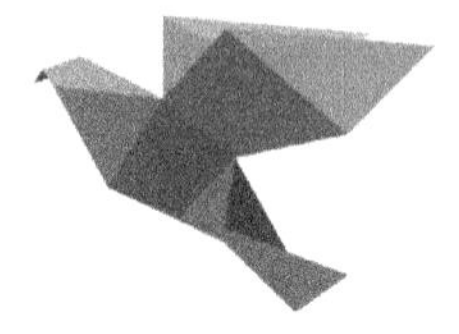

CHAPTER 9

Unbroken: A Story of Addiction, Relapse, and Recovery
Carly Ellman, PhD, LCSW

I woke up again, filled with dread, wondering, *What did I do last night? What did I say to my husband and kids?* My head sank into my hands because I couldn't even bring myself to look in the mirror. I felt completely exhausted—mentally, physically, emotionally—and drowning in shame. The weight of it was unbearable, and in that moment, I realized something had to change. I couldn't keep living this way.

Let's be honest—my life was a mess—a spectacular, flaming, five-alarm disaster. I hated myself. I hated how I felt every morning, piecing together foggy memories from the night before like some deranged detective in my own sad mystery novel. I was starring in the role of "the woman who can't get it together," and believe me, it was not a glamorous part. On the outside, though, I could hold it all together—working multiple jobs, showing up for my family, and doing it well. But inside? I was crumbling. And the worst part was—I didn't even know who I was without the drinking, the chaos, and the constant noise in my head.

This is my story of recovery. It is deeply personal, and it's important for me to share the truth of my struggles, relapses, and the lessons I've learned, in hopes that others might better understand the reality of these battles—and the incredible beauty of life in recovery. My journey through alcoholism and an eating disorder has taught me several essential truths, which I share below:

1. Alcoholism and eating disorders are diseases. They consume your thoughts and energy, leaving you a shell of yourself. I wouldn't wish them on anyone.

2. Recovery is possible, though it takes daily work and support—you do not have to do it alone.

3. Relapse does not mean failure. It simply means you need more help or different tools.

4. The decision to recover must come from within. No outside force—not family, friends, or work—can force lasting sobriety.

5. Sobriety doesn't erase life's difficulties, but it gives you the strength and clarity to face anything. And yes, life in recovery is worth it.

If you have ever listened to people's stories at an AA meeting, mine starts similarly. I grew up with a void inside myself. I never felt like I was enough or a part of a family or group. Both of my parents' first marriages failed, and they made it their mission to ensure their marriage to each other would work. To me, it felt like their marriage was the priority, not me, and my needs would never get in the way of their love for each other. I literally spent most of my free time as a child, both weekend nights, with a babysitter.

It wasn't until sixth grade, on a crisp fall afternoon, that I first felt like I belonged anywhere. I had just joined the field hockey team, and as I stepped onto the field in my oversized jersey and borrowed shin guards, something shifted. The weight of never quite fitting in—at home, at school, even in my own body—seemed a little lighter. I had always felt different: shorter than most girls, curvier in a way that made me stand out in uncomfortable ways, especially to boys. Clothes didn't fit right, and whispers from peers often stung more than I let on. But out there, running drills with my teammates, I was just another athlete.

Field hockey became more than a sport—it was my lifeline. For the next nine years, it grounded me, offering structure, purpose, and the chance to be part of something bigger than myself. I stayed away from drinking in high school, partly out of fear of getting into trouble and partly because I didn't want anything to interfere with the one thing that made me feel whole. My older half-brother was the one known for partying—he always seemed to get away with it. When I eventually got sober, I often asked myself, "How did I become the one with the problem?" It wasn't until college that alcohol entered the picture in a meaningful way. Off the field and away from the discipline of the season, drinking with teammates became a way to belong all over again—just in a different, more dangerous form.

I had my first blackout freshman year, and it scared me, but not enough for me to stop drinking. I studied abroad in Rome as a sophomore, where wine was cheaper than water. It was easy to eat and drink excessively in Italy, and I gained a lot of weight. When I got home, I wanted to stop playing field hockey and transfer to another school. I have always feared financial insecurity, and this moment remains a core memory: My parents told me they would support me in transferring, but I would need to pay anything above the cost of state tuition since I would be leaving a scholarship. So, what did I do? I stayed, and I hated it and myself.

Around this time, I started some unhealthy eating routines, drank a little more, and even smoked some pot. I enjoyed pot more at this point because I could eat whatever I wanted and wouldn't feel guilty (the feeling I eventually got from drinking alcohol).

My mom was, and continues to be, very conscious and obsessive about her appearance and eating. When I was growing up, my mom restricted foods, and I remember my dad sneaking snacks when she wasn't around. Watching my mom's habits created in me a very unhealthy relationship with food and body image, and my relationships (both with body image and my mom) remain toxic to this day.

In the summer before my senior year, I figured out how to purge my food. This was the worst thing I ever learned, although at the time it felt like a golden ticket. I lost weight and got my first real boyfriend since high school. He was a college dropout living in Arizona, teaching golf, and doing drugs. I was smitten. He moved home in the fall of my senior year and lived on his friend's floor on an air mattress. Every time we hung out, I was drinking, and he was smoking. I went back to school in the spring of my senior year, purging, drinking, and depressed. Halfway through the semester, I convinced my parents I needed help with the eating disorder so I could move home. My parents knew about my eating struggles, but they didn't know how bad it was until I called from college. According to the eating disorder treatment intake assessment, I was not sick enough for inpatient treatment, so I went to outpatient treatment. I finished my senior spring semester on my own, working individually with my professors to meet course requirements, while going to an outpatient treatment program during the day and drinking with my boyfriend at night.

The following spring, I started my Master's in Social Work. I was doing great in school and loved every moment of the next two and a half years as a social work student and graduate assistant. Around that time, my parents sold my childhood home, retired, and moved to Rhode Island and then eventually to Florida. As a result, I was forced to move out and find roommates. That is when I bought a case of wine, which I kept in my car and brought in one bottle a night to drink alone in my room (one bottle eventually turned into two). I was also still losing weight in an unhealthy way, privately eating the food that I wanted, which my mom had forbidden me from doing when I was growing up. After graduating and getting my first job in February of 2011, I finally went into treatment in Florida because my eating disorder and alcoholism were both out of control. I told myself the only reason I got into the program was that I lied and said I drank more than I did (which was less than I truly was drinking). It was there that I first learned about AA. I was there for sixty-three days. I got healthy physically and mentally. I moved back to the area where I grew up and started going to AA meetings, but I felt super young and could not relate to my fellow AA members and the culture. I also did not believe I was an alcoholic.

My eating seemed to be under control until one day, while at work, I swallowed a plastic fork. I didn't know what to do, so I ignored it at first, but soon realized I needed medical attention. I went to the hospital, where they took an X-ray, which showed nothing, so they sent me home. I eventually went back because I was scared; I was going to die. They did deeper testing and finally found the fork. I was put on suicide watch because they thought I was trying to kill myself. I didn't think I was suicidal, but perhaps subconsciously, I was. They surgically removed the fork, and I was sent to my parents' house in Rhode Island for a few days. I started going back to AA, but then stopped. I still did not believe drinking was my problem.

I met my husband on December 30, 2011. He did not know any of this history and did not learn of my eating disorder until after we were engaged. He thought my eating habits were a bit strange, but he had no experience with eating disorders, so he took it at face value. He did not learn about my drinking problem until three months after our first daughter was born.

We dated long-distance for six months, and then I moved to his hometown and started a life there. All the while, I was unhealthy and drinking more than I let on. He told me after I got sober that I would make him feel bad if he didn't drink with me. Eventually, I found myself hiding my drinks from him. I would drink a decent amount before we went out, have one or two drinks while out, and then drink in the bathroom back at home. He couldn't figure out why a second glass of wine often put me over the edge, not knowing he only saw two out of many.

At our wedding, I was drunk, and the wedding planner ensured I had my own bottle of Riesling right next to my seat at all times. One night, I was so intoxicated at dinner with friends that I ate two loaves of bread, passed out at the table, and later convinced my husband that the waiter had drugged me. I hate myself for thinking of all these lies.

I hadn't had a drink in almost a year—throughout my pregnancy and the first four weeks of my daughter's life. But once I started again, it was like flipping a switch I couldn't turn off.

The days at home were long. I was alone with a newborn, exhausted and drowning in postpartum depression, and I didn't yet have the language to describe. The quiet in the house was deafening. I'd walk the halls with her in my arms, desperate to soothe her—and myself. When the bottle called, it whispered promises of calm, of control, of escape.

On January 20, 2016, it all came undone.

It was dark out when I decided to run down the street to pick up dinner. I told myself I deserved a break, just one glass of wine at the bar while I waited. I can still remember the feel of the stem between my fingers, the cold smoothness of the glass. The wine was crisp and familiar—too familiar.

The rest is a blur.

The following image is seared into my mind: flashing lights, a smashed-up front porch, and my car angled crookedly in someone else's living room. I blinked hard, trying to make sense of what I was seeing. My hands were shaking, my mouth dry. The realization came in waves: I had no idea how I got there. I had no memory of leaving the restaurant. The guilt hit fast and hard, like my body had sucker-punched me.

I was arrested on the spot.

At the hospital, I remember Joe's eyes—wide, scared, confused—and the small bundle he held in his arms. Our daughter was only three months old. I couldn't even bring myself to look at her. The shame was too heavy.

I went to AA the next day. Sat in a metal chair under fluorescent lights and listened to strangers tell stories that sounded far too familiar. For the first time, I said the words out loud: *I'm an alcoholic.*

And I meant them—until I didn't.

I worked through an excellent program. I attended meetings every day, worked with my sponsor, did the steps, and got into service. My life became so much better, beyond my wildest dreams. I had another daughter, became an assistant professor, started a private practice, and did not think about or want to drink. AA had become my new normal. Most of my friends were in the program, and I really thought this would be my life forever.

My eating disorder was always closely tied to my alcoholism. During these six years of sobriety, I have been freed from my eating disorder. Covid hit, and I did online meetings, and still, drinking did not entice me.

We moved to the Philadelphia suburbs in December 2020, full of hope for a fresh start. The house was bigger, the schools were great, and the neighborhood was beautiful—but inside, I felt untethered.

The shame crept in quietly. I didn't tell anyone in our new town that I was in recovery. I told myself it was for privacy, but deep down, I was afraid of judgment. Recovery had always been something I carried with quiet pride, but now, in a world where no one knew my past, it became something I hid.

We joined a country club not long after we moved in. That's where I met them—the moms in tennis skirts and blowouts, laughing with white wine in hand, as if life never got messy for them. Even the kids' swim practices and tennis lessons had wine service. Sip and Serve, they called it. I'd sit on the bleachers with my water bottle and pretend I didn't notice how easy it looked for everyone else.

They made it look glamorous—rosé in the sunshine, cocktails after doubles matches, champagne at charity events. I'd smile and nod and laugh along, but inside I was tense, watching every pour, timing how long it took each woman to finish her glass. I studied them the way I used to study textbooks—searching for answers. *How do they do it? How do they stop?*

All I wanted was to belong. To be invited. To be included.

That summer, I stayed sober, but it was like white-knuckling a rollercoaster. I fixated on the drinks around me, on how effortlessly these women seemed to blend motherhood, social life, and indulgence. I believed that maybe I had outgrown my alcoholism, that perhaps it had just been a phase.

In the fall, while writing my qualifying paper for my Ph.D., I was told I passed. Relief washed over me. But days later, I got another email—there had been a mistake. I had actually failed. The floor dropped out from under me. I felt humiliated and isolated. I spiraled, replaying the judgment I imagined from my professors, the whispering I projected onto those country club moms.

In January 2022, just days before my six-year sober anniversary, I walked into the local wine shop and bought a bottle. I stood in the kitchen holding it, my hands trembling slightly, and told my husband, "I just want to be normal. I just want to fit in."

I told myself it would be different this time, that I could be the kind of woman who sips wine in the sun and stops after one.

But deep down, I already knew that wasn't who I was.

He didn't know what to do, but there was also really nothing he could do. So, that night, I had a glass of wine. By the next night at 10 p.m., I was alone downstairs drinking wine out of my daughter's water bottle. That is how fast I reverted to full-blown alcoholism. It felt so good, but also so terrible. I started drinking often, would black out, and do and say stupid things. I was hiding wine all over the house and never went anywhere without it. I was scaring my kids by yelling and then passing out. I even jumped on a few AA Zoom meetings drunk.

What made this relapse even harder was that this time, my husband knew. I thought I was great at being sneaky, but he always knew. He could tell from my breath and my speech. I exhausted myself trying to keep it a secret, but it was all for nothing. I wasn't getting away with anything. He sat me down for countless conversations, asking me to get help and stop drinking.

That summer, I went to a five-day yoga, meditation, and recovery workshop. I remember my father-in-law calling it treatment, and that pissed me off. It was an enlightening experience, though, and I left feeling energetic about sobriety. When I returned home, I began attending AA meetings in my area. It was then that I started the process of "coming in and out." When I was sober the first time, I never understood why people would leave and drink, and now I get it because this disease is the worst, and it wants us dead. I got 18 days, drank 20 days, drank 30 days, drank four days, and drank and drank. This endless cycle was literal hell. I was so unhappy with every aspect of my life, and I could not stop drinking. I was half in and half out of the program. I would go to meetings, but only those that fit my schedule. I would not move things around or put AA or my sobriety first. I justified this by saying I couldn't, that I had to work and make money (more lies).

Finally, on Sunday, January 8, 2023, I had been sober for 4 days and went to a 10:15 a.m. meeting after my daughter's soccer game. It was a great meeting, but I sat there planning to stop at the liquor store on my way home. Over this past year, I went from drinking wine to drinking vodka because I thought it didn't smell and was easier to hide. More lies this disease told me. So, instead of speaking up and asking for help, I stopped and bought alcohol and was drunk by the time I got home. We had my in-laws and my husband's uncle at the house. I was drunk and don't remember most of it, but I made a scene. I woke up in the morning, got the girls off to school, and sat on the couch with my husband, having the same conversation about my drinking being a problem that we had had about fifty times in the past year. He asked, "What are we going to do?" For some reason, I said, "I think I need to go to rehab." Why I said it that day, I will never know, but I am so grateful I did.

I contacted a woman I had become friendly with in AA and asked for help. She made some calls, and I was in rehab later that morning. I went to my daughter's school to tell them I was going to the hospital for a little while. It was devastating and heartbreaking. I cried all through the hospital intake and the following week. I was so uncomfortable. Being in rehab was the worst sixteen days of my life, but the experience of being an inpatient also saved my life. It made me realize that if I did not stop drinking, I would die, lose everything, or end up back there.

A friend in AA had told me to pray for the obsession to drink to be lifted. Prayer was not a big part of my program, either during my previous time in sobriety or while I was in and out, but this time, I was willing to try it. I was the only person who did not smoke at rehab, so I would walk around the building for thirty minutes multiple times a day and ask God to remove my obsession with drinking. Still today, nineteen months sober, this is part of my daily plan. When I left rehab, I went right to a meeting and have gone every day since. I started making AA and sobriety the most important things in my life. More important than my family and my job, because if I am not sober, I lose all of that.

I have a new sponsor, a woman who I saw handle a complex situation with dignity and grace. We meet weekly and speak daily. I also try to call other women to ask how they are doing. My life has become much fuller and easier to manage. The world around me hadn't changed—but I had. My motivation was different. I finally wanted to stop, not just for others, but for myself. I still have all the same life situations that bother me, but I have a program and a higher power to help me get through without thinking about a drink. I thank my higher power every day for helping me not to drink. I also have a fantastic support system through my family and AA. I know firsthand what happens when I pick up a drink: my life becomes a mess, and I want to die. Today I do not want to die. Today I feel happy, sad, joyful, anxious, and many other feelings that I do not need to numb. I allow myself to feel all the emotions that are a part of life.

Being sober and in recovery is a GIFT.

Alcoholism and eating disorders are diseases. I would not wish these afflictions on my worst enemy. When in the grips of these diseases, they change who you are as a person and who you can be. They occupy all your thoughts and brainpower, turning you into a shell of a person.

Recovery from both *is* possible. It requires daily hard work, but you can do it, and you do not have to do it alone.

Sometimes people relapse: that does not mean they are failures or that the program they were working on was a failure. It means they need more help.

The desire to be sober or in recovery must come solely from within. There is nothing or no one, not husbands, wives, kids, parents, jobs, etc., that can get someone sober. We need support around us, but ultimately, the decision to get sober rests with the individual.

A sober life still has all the daily stresses, huge losses, sadness, anxiety, and depression, but being sober, we can handle anything that comes our way. A sober life is wonderful!

Carly Ellman, PhD, LCSW

Carly Ellman, PhD, LCSW, is an experienced clinician, educator, and leader in the field of social work and sports mental health. She holds a PhD in Strategic Leadership and Administration from Marywood University and a Master's in Social Work (MSW) from Fordham University. She is a Licensed Clinical Social Worker in both Pennsylvania and Florida.

Dr. Ellman currently serves as an assistant professor of social work and program coordinator at Delaware County Community College. She previously held the role of assistant professor of medicine at Geisinger Commonwealth School of Medicine. In addition to her academic leadership, Carly maintains a thriving private practice in Dresher, Pennsylvania, where she works with adolescents, college students, and adults navigating life transitions, anxiety, depression, and eating disorders.

Deeply committed to athlete mental health, Carly works with athletes across all levels to support performance and well-being. She is a certified sports social worker through the Association of Social Work in Sports and Tulane University. Currently, she serves as a consultant for the

United States Olympic and Paralympic Committee, providing mental health training and clinical services.

Carly is the secretary of the National Association of Social Workers (NASW) and is actively involved in advancing the profession through training and advocacy. Outside of her professional life, Carly enjoys coaching youth field hockey and spending quality time with her husband Joe and their three daughters—Gianna, Aubrey, and Maya.

CHAPTER 10

The Grand Optimist
Jared Lombardi, MSW, LSW, DRCC

I was twelve years old when I first thought about death. I didn't have a secure attachment to my parents and felt emotionally neglected throughout childhood; I found comfort in isolation and created a safe space in the dark corner of my bedroom closet. I didn't realize then that the darkness I surrounded myself with mirrored what I felt inside. Knowing that no one is coming to save you is worse than sitting in the darkness alone.

My father worked as an accountant, and my mother stayed home to care for us, but neither presence eased the ache of loneliness. Instead, my early sense of the world was shaped by family members on my mother's side who struggled with substance use. I remember their blank stares, the chemically induced smiles, and their slurred speech.

My mother completed high school and moved to work in the casino business in Atlantic City, where she met my father. Unfortunately, she didn't move far enough away from her family, and as a result, she was unable to start anew. Being so close to the shore, our house became a place for our misguided family members to stay. Parental conflict was prevalent in my family, impacting the children and leading to aggression, delinquency, and behavioral issues. Our cousins bullied my brother and me when we were young during family gatherings. Looking back, I realized my cousins identified with their parents' behavior at home. In my childhood, I would feel anxious whenever the phone rang at home because family members would call to discuss a family member's overdose or relapse, psychological suffering, domestic violence, and make hostile remarks toward my mother.

I was bullied from childhood through young adulthood, which targeted my low self-esteem and lack of self-worth, escalating over the years and diminishing my will to live. I knew my grandparents had passed away from old age, but I was focused on expediting that process for myself. Puberty brought chaos to my mental health, leading to increased anxiety, stress, and suicidal thoughts. Mental health support was lacking due to family dynamics and bullying, which affected my school performance. My teachers would sometimes yell at me because they thought I had done something to make the students laugh, but the students were not laughing with me; they were laughing at me.

Growing up, my father's strong work ethic gave our family a comfortable home and all the essentials needed to raise a healthy family. We were fortunate to have food in our kitchen, clothes on our backs, holiday gifts, and even vacations to Disney World. However, one day in 2005, a loud knock was at the door while I was at home with my father. My mother was at the grocery store with my brother and sister. My dad entered my room in a panic, holding a trash bag. He told me the sheriff's department was at the door and that I needed to quickly pack a bag with only the items I wanted to keep because we were being evicted from our home. He instructed me to then move on to my brother and sister's room after I was done choosing my items to pack some of their things. After a long conversation with the officers outside our home, my father returned and told me we would be allowed to stay and that I could unpack my stuff. However, he advised me to remember the items I had collected if this situation happened again. I trusted my father, but I was confused about what had just happened, and I was never given an explanation for why it happened while I stood there with a trash bag full of my childhood possessions.

Following the visit to our home by the sheriff's officers and during my senior year of high school, my depression worsened, suicidal thoughts increased, and I started to leave class so I could experience my panic attacks alone in the bathroom stall. I didn't want to show my classmates any more weakness; they would continue to use it against me. Throughout the school year, I found motivation to pass my classes because graduation was a step closer to ending my life. During my high school graduation ceremony, I was not proud of my academic achievement, and the focus was now on building the courage within myself to end my life. I was creative in my planning and looked toward death through the lethal consumption of alcohol. My family being active members of the Catholic faith influenced my choice not to express my suicidal ideation due to the stigma that surrounded suicide and the shame and guilt my parents would have to endure when word came out that I took my own life. The Catholic faith states that hell is best understood as the condition of total alienation from all that is good, hopeful, and loving in the world, but it was never told to me that you could enter hell while still alive.

Entering college, I planned to become another statistic of reckless behavior. Overconsumption of alcohol on college campuses was expected, and death by alcohol was possible. In October 2006, my first year of college, I obtained a handle of vodka illegally from a co-worker. I drank the entire bottle in twenty minutes, celebrating as if reaching the finish line not of a race but of my life. Thoughts of relief passed through my mind, and I accepted that this was how my life was meant to end. My next memory was opening my eyes to a nurse handing me a phone with my father on the other line, asking, "Are you okay?" The words that should have come out of my mouth were that I was not okay and that I had just tried to kill myself, but those words were distant. I was recovering from the lethal consumption of alcohol, blocking my brain from accessing rational thought. I told my father that I was okay.

The one thing I didn't plan for was failing at ending my life and the dark path it would continue to lead me down. I built up the courage and created the plan, but it wasn't good enough. I went to church shortly after my attempt and asked God, "Why am I still alive?" Due to my suicide plan being attached to alcohol, I was charged with underage drinking, and the university put me on probation. I met with a school psychologist, and she was more focused on alcohol misuse than the underlying psychological pain that led me to drink a lethal amount. I was told that campus security saw me on surveillance, stumbling into the surrounding neighborhood. They found me collapsed on the side of the road without a pulse. My father kept this information from my mother due to the potential consequences. Little did my father know I was already dealing with the consequences, and I entered a downward spiral of self-medicating through substance use. I had two goals: one was building up the courage to attempt suicide a second time, and the other was making enough money to sustain my active substance use. I surrounded myself with individuals who supported my bad habits, not my recovery. My time in college was stressful overall, as my college roommate physically abused me, and I didn't attend classes because my focus was on ending my life instead of achieving academic success.

In 2007, after I dropped out of college, my father was sentenced to four years in prison for deceptive business practices. I remember visiting him with my sister and buying him peanut M&M's from the vending machine because it would put a smile on his face. Later, I realized the smile was created by his children, who came to sit with him in the darkness, helping to shine a light. I felt empathy towards my father's situation because I felt like I was serving a prison sentence in my head. After my attempt, I thought about talking to my dad, but before I could build the strength to speak, he was in prison. I felt it was a sign not to open up to him because who would want to hear about their son's suicide attempt while sitting in a prison cell?

We were evicted from our home in 2008 after my father was released from prison, and he served the rest of his sentence on probation. With the uncertainty of my life's possessions, we spent days filling rental PODS, unsure of our destination and why this was happening. I spent time in the woods behind our home contemplating another attempt to take my life, but I was resistant because I didn't want to leave my family when they needed help packing and relocating. The court had given my father a deadline to vacate the property, but I had no idea it would be the last time I would see the items I had painstakingly packed into those PODS. I was never told by my parents where the PODS went, but what I did know was that every positive keepsake and memory from my childhood disappeared that day, and my suicidal thoughts grew stronger. At that moment, I would tell myself, 'Be patient: it will all be over soon.'

After being removed from our home, my parents did their best with what they had. During that time, we found out that my father was diagnosed with pancreatic cancer and was developing tumors in both his colon and lungs. My parents faced difficulties getting approved for a mortgage due to my father's criminal record and financial situation; we bounced around from short winter rentals to hotel rooms in the summer months. My parents did everything they could to keep a roof over our heads, while I did everything I could to try to distance myself from them by couch surfing and sleeping in my car. I didn't want to confront the fact that, after all the trauma my family faced, we would now watch my father suffer from the symptoms of his cancer before his life came to an early end.

I remember when we were staying in a hotel outside of Atlantic City, and my father's colostomy bag broke off his port and sprayed all over the bathroom. I heard his laughter, so I entered the bathroom because the door was cracked. I saw him laughing at the pain he was going through, as he realized how terrible his life had become.

Once again, these moments of trauma instilled hope in me to continue to live so I wouldn't make my father's life any worse. After years of relocating, sleeping on floors, couches, and air mattresses, we finally found a home to move into, and that would be where my father found peace to take his last breath in November 2013. My father didn't show me much affection throughout my life, so when my mother notified me he had passed away in his sleep, I made sure to hug him and kiss him on the forehead. Even though his affection wasn't a lasting memory, it would be our last.

Following my father's death, non-suicidal self-injury (NSSI), also known as self-harm, entered my toxic plan for further self-destruction. My emotional suffering had led me to the compulsive behavior patterns of substance use and self-harm. I attributed my self-harm to emotional distress, underlying but undiagnosed mental health disorders, trauma history, social and environmental factors, and self-punishment, but most importantly, it provided relief to my mental health. My preferred method of self-harm was cutting because I felt it was helping me practice for when I built up the courage to cut through a vein. My alcohol misuse would lead me to smash my head into walls and put lit cigarettes out on my skin to punish myself for feeling like a failure and unworthy of life. Being emotionally neglected as a child made me lack focus on others' emotions while not being able to regulate my own. I prioritized the compulsion to self-harm so much that I entered relationships with women who could resonate with the behavior or tolerate it. During this time, one girlfriend regularly hid the butcher block knives in my house to keep me from self-harming. At times, I would be out at the bar bleeding through one of my shirts while I sat there numb to the world, searching for an end. It was a way to communicate feelings without words, but I surrounded myself with individuals who minimized my trauma and found the act to be attention-seeking. I had gotten to a point where the act of self-harm had caused stronger cravings than substances did.

As the scars became more noticeable, I turned to tattoos to help cover them up while also providing me with the same relief because it was a more acceptable way of self-harm. My first tattoo was the Grim Reaper because death was the only figure of belief that represented my internal thoughts while masking my emotional cues.

My priority of substance use led me to work at a local bar, which supported my bad habits. I surrounded myself with friends who exhibited the same behavior as the toxic family members that I had detached myself from. A red flag doesn't feel like a red flag when it feels like home. Almost every shift I worked, I was under the influence of substances, but I was praised for my hard work. I spent my days off misusing substances at my workplace. I would sit at the crowded bar feeling alone, focused on which parking garage to jump from, which red light to ride my bike through, or which bathtub to use as my final resting place. The bar was my workplace, home, prison, drug dealer, therapist, enabler, toxic support, and false hope. After my shifts, I would often find myself on the streets of Atlantic City alone at 5 a.m., hoping to encounter someone who could guide me toward death. When I was let go from my job because of my unstable behavior and substance misuse, the bar manager told me I would never get better and that I would continue down the path of addiction, just like she had seen in her past employees. You can't build a different life in the same environment that's holding you back.

Up until 2018, I had aborted over a dozen suicide attempts due to unexpected social interactions. In 2018, I fell down the back steps of a local bar because of my alcohol misuse, hitting my head, which led me to suffer a subdural hemorrhage. I hit rock bottom. I was in a coma for two days and in the ICU for a week. The incident caused me to lose my relationship with my brother, who saw me as an addict. I asked God once again, "Why am I still alive?" After leaving the hospital, I started drinking and misusing substances within two days. My friend, who recently was in crisis care for suicidal thoughts, saw the warning signs and took me by the hand to seek help. At that moment, I felt acknowledged, valued, and supported. I was diagnosed with post-traumatic stress disorder and obsessive-compulsive personality disorder in the program. The following year, I regularly attended a behavioral health treatment program. I built a positive support system, removed myself from toxic relationships and environments, stayed sober, advocated for suicide prevention, and met my soulmate, who made me feel deserving of love. Most importantly, I began to love myself for the first time. I was surrounded by people who genuinely cared about me and my recovery.

As I embraced this new life where I felt loved and loved myself, I unfortunately was involved in a motor vehicle accident. In June 2020, I was rear-ended while stopped at a traffic light. This collision led to my second traumatic brain injury in less than three years and permanent spinal cord damage. Now, being in recovery, I had two options: one was to relapse and ruin all the progress I had made, or see this accident as a reminder of the strength I had to move forward. While recovering, I had to leave my former career because I could no longer meet the job requirements. In the following year of treatment and rehabilitation, my cognitive therapist referred me to the Division of Vocational Rehabilitation, which provided me with the funding to attend an educational facility that would allow me to pursue my life's purpose. My first experience at college in 2006 was the first time I attempted to kill myself, so being allowed to attend college again was a second chance at living the life that had stayed in my dreams but was never seen as a reality.

Over the following three years, the answer to the question, "Why am I still alive?" revealed itself. I completed my bachelor's and master's degrees in social work at Stockton University, maintaining a 4.0 GPA and earning distinction in both programs, while remaining committed to my sobriety. I married my soulmate, and we now have a beautiful baby girl with the middle name of Hope. I succeeded through self-discipline, self-love, and a supportive network. However, I worked to achieve it by accepting my past, adopting a growth mindset, and finding value in the treatment process.

In 2019, I founded The Positive Pursuit to share positivity and hope with individuals in the community who encounter mental health challenges. With the community's help, over 10,000 sunflowers have been distributed to instill hope and remind us of our strength, even in our weakest moments, to reach out for help. Reminiscent of recovery, sunflowers grow toward the sun, leaving the darkness behind them. Providing life-saving discussions and services in my community has given me the strength to keep moving forward and confidently state that there is always hope. Start the conversation and check in with your loved ones because it could save a life. I know it saved mine.

Jared Lombardi, MSW, LSW, DRCC

Jared Lombardi, MSW, LSW, DRCC, is a mental health advocate and community activist who founded The Positive Pursuit in 2019. The organization aims to raise awareness about suicide prevention and promote healing and hope in the community.

Jared seeks to reverse current trends in suicide deaths and drug overdoses while reducing the stigma associated with getting help for one's mental health and substance use. The strategic initiatives he implements aim to connect community members with life-saving resources and instill hope in vulnerable populations.

Jared feels immense gratitude toward his wife, Savannah, and his supportive friends and family, who have served as his guiding lights. This chapter is dedicated to his beautiful daughter, Maeve Hope, born on September 4, 2024.

"Love is just a tool to remind us of who we are and that we are not alone when walking in the dark."

Instagram: the_positive_pursuit
Facebook: The Positive Pursuit
LinkedIn: Jared Lombardi, MSW, LSW, DRCC

CHAPTER 11

Bending with the Storm: Resilience in Recovery
Douglas Achtert, MSS, LCSW

My pain truly started once I recovered, but my story began like everyone else who goes down this path, or at least damn close to it, with pain that knows no bounds screaming from the inside. I was lonely and depressed, and I didn't like who I was, so I found something that took me out of who I was. But this isn't about the drugs I used or the alcohol I drank; this is about recovery. This involves my story, but it's not just about me. Recovery is more than simply quitting the addiction. It's about building resilience—facing the daily trials, coping with the losses, and moving through the lives ahead of you.

In high school, I faced internal emotional struggles due to undiagnosed bipolar disorder, which led me down this path as I tried to cope on my own. I bounced from counselor to counselor, none of whom seemed to have anything to offer me. Eventually, one seemed like he could handle what I was going through, but even he referred me to a psychiatrist. I felt broken, different, and destined to be misunderstood forever. With this new psychiatrist, however, I felt seen and understood. The missing pieces seemed to come together, and I began to find the support I needed through counseling. This allowed me to take steps toward recovery from the pills, the drink, and anything else I could find to help ease the pain.

Unfortunately, this progress was short-lived. Within a few months, I slipped, caught a case, and checked myself into rehab. It all happened when an old friend and I went to a concert—a reunion of half of Led Zeppelin. Without thinking, we started off the evening getting high, and it only went downhill from there. Walking through the venue, we found harder and harder drugs that we used throughout the night. When I got home, I crashed, but it didn't stop there. I woke up, kept using, and went to school. Once at school, my friends became concerned about my well-being as they suspected I had relapsed. I was called to the office, and the dean looked at me, simply stating, "Has anything happened in the past twenty-four hours that would lead your friends to be worried about you?" I paused and reflected on my options: try to lead an open and honest life, or continue down the path that brought me more and more pain. I quickly decided that it was time, and that led to my sharing my experience in the office of the mass quantities of narcotics used by me over the previous day. That's when the cops were called, and I ended up with a citation and a court date later in the year. It also led me to an honest conversation with my psychiatrist and a referral to an inpatient facility that evening. This is where my actual work began.

I got into real recovery at seventeen, and it wasn't exactly smooth sailing. I was young, worn out, and pissed off. It seemed like no one else had any problems. I was frustrated watching others go off to college to enjoy a "normal" social life. Meanwhile, for my first year after high school, I ended up at Vassar. It was there that I found I couldn't concentrate because the antidepressants my psychiatrist prescribed kept me up all night. I was in a manic state and didn't even realize it. Another psychiatrist diagnosed me with bipolar disorder without telling me and put me on a mood stabilizer. I hated the combo of meds—I felt like a zombie—so I promptly took myself off of both. I was supported in these turbulent times by the friends I met at college orientation. I will never forget the words of my friend Erin, who one night pulled me aside and said, "Doug, you are so much better of a person than you let yourself be; start being that person." At this time, I was also asked not to return to school after just one semester, with a GPA of 0.25. After these disheartening experiences, I knew I needed a change of pace.

Returning home seemed like a setback, but it turned out to be a step in the right direction. I dove deeper and deeper into punk, into the hardcore subculture. I started going to shows as often as I could. It was a safe space for my anger to fester. I was that asshole—the one who would kick the joint out of your hand if you lit it up in the venue, or knock the beer out of your hand on the dancefloor, staring you down deadpan, daring you to fight. Am I proud of this? No. But being in that environment, surrounded by that music, gave me more than an outlet for my violence and anger. I found a sense of belonging there, seeing some people from high school, namely Mikey, who was a few years older, and most of the new friends I was with were there for the same reason I was, because that belonging wasn't there where they grew up. It was here that my intensity was recognized and accepted, where I felt accepted. This chaotic environment, oddly enough, became a stepping stone toward finding inner peace, as I found myself in a culture where standing up for others, introspection, and spiritual balance were found at the outskirts.

Slowly, the dust settled, and I entered a new, quieter chapter. That's where my life sat for a few years. I eventually got back into another school after establishing a semblance of routine by working and attending community college for a year and a half. I found a girlfriend and made new friends, seeing my support through good people and music. There was something in the lyrics that I sang along with—a yearning, a sense of justice, a search for hope. I could only physically fight for my recovery for so long before I realized I needed to find a better way.

After graduation, things were going well. My girlfriend and I were living together, I loved my job, and I had been in recovery for nearly eight years. I was still unmedicated since college, and everything seemed great. Until it didn't. My life hit a wall—I messed up in my relationship, was told to move out, and I mentally broke down. Those first few months were brutal, and it was solely my fault. My girlfriend told me I had to break up with her so I couldn't put any of the blame on her. It spiraled me into a period of self-hatred, of flagellation. I wasn't sleeping or eating; I couldn't focus on work, and I was constantly crying. I just couldn't pull myself together. Morning and night, I journaled to get the painful thoughts out of my head. I needed an escape—something to soothe me and comfort me. But I didn't go back to drugs.

Instead, I turned to literature. I began reading voraciously, searching for an answer, any answer that would bring me closer to peace. As I tore through book after book, I noticed a pattern. Titles like *When Things Fall Apart*, *Anger: Wisdom for Cooling the Flames*, and *The Art of Happiness* drew me in. It took me longer than it should have to realize that all these books were leading me to the same place: Buddhism, and more specifically, meditation.

So, I sat down and started to meditate. I attended meditation centers in the city, taking day-long trainings and retreats just to learn how to be with my breath and accept the present moment. I found communities— and then I saw *my* community. A crew of swearing, tattooed punks, all trying to let go of their anger and find their contentment, just like me. Sure, I found my community in New York City, but what was a four-hour round-trip drive from Philadelphia in exchange for finding happiness?

I dove in headfirst, sitting in meditation daily. I attended my first five-day silent retreat, followed by another month-long silent retreat in California. Meditation became more than just a hobby; it became my practice, my daily requirement, an integral part of my life. I knew the answers I sought were out there, and I was determined to put in the work to find them.

Despite finding meditation, however, my inner fears still lingered. My biggest worry was that if people truly got to know me, they wouldn't want me in their lives. It sounded ridiculous to me, too! It felt ridiculous. But it also felt real—justified by my life experience. This fear is what kept me closed off, why I kept my ever-fluctuating thoughts to myself. I didn't think my range of emotions was any more intense than anyone else's, but I've heard, more times than I'd like to admit, "I'm sorry, you're just too much for me to handle." I never knew what to do with those words.

I wanted to trust, to be open and vulnerable, to show the world what was in my heart. But for as long as I could remember, I felt like I'd been told—by others and my own inner voice—that my feelings weren't valid. That there was something "wrong" with me, that people just didn't know how to deal with having me in their lives. Through years of meditation after my breakup, I'd done some serious work on my trust issues. I'd taken great strides and made real progress—I just felt it. But it was still hard to open up and truly learn to trust. I kept worrying that people would look at me differently once they knew the real me. I often heard that I needed to take time for myself, to spend time alone. Yet, some part of me always felt alone, hiding fragments of myself just to feel a bit connected.

Then, something changed—I started to trust. Through my meditation practice and the insight gained through constant reading, I lessened my need to control and gave others a chance. I finally opened up, let people know what was on my mind, and found that I wasn't ostracized. I had found community and was outwardly accepted as myself, but still waited for the other shoe to drop, feeling even more alone at times. I was afraid of angering someone or making them uncomfortable, even though I knew I shouldn't let those worries control me. But the truth was, my actions and words *did* affect others. These fears left me feeling more confused, more disconnected, and more alone than ever.

Around this time, I faced two painful losses that pushed me to reflect on connections. During this period of upheaval and searching, I heard about Erin, a friend from my first year of college. Throughout that semester, we often talked and hung out; she was really there for me when I needed support the most. When I left, I lost contact with almost everyone—mainly because I had been without internet access for 2 years. So, life went on, and years later, I was working as a messenger, receiving occasional updates from the alumni association.

Then came that fateful July. I checked my email and burst into tears. Driving home after a night out with friends, Erin fell asleep at the wheel and died. We hadn't spoken in eight years, as this was before cell phones and the internet were as ubiquitous as they are now, but I knew I needed to be there. Flights were too expensive, and my car could barely make it around the block. So, I rented a car, took a long weekend from work, and drove north. Many people had gathered to commemorate her remarkable life, and there I was—overcome with sadness that I hadn't known her well enough.

This was the first friend's death that struck me this way. I'd lost friends before—to overdoses, car accidents, and other tragedies—and while it was always a shame, Erin's death hit differently. My specific response to Erin's death was that *I should have known her better.* And dwelling on that, of course, did no good. You can't negotiate for more time, and you can never change what has happened in the past, no matter how hard you wish you could.

I felt like I'd been doing better, connecting with people on a deeper level, when another tragedy reignited my self-doubt. Mikey passed away senselessly. He was struck by a drunk driver while walking home. Mikey was someone else I didn't know nearly well enough, mainly because of my own insecurities. Most people knew Mikey for his involvement in the music scene; he sang in several bands around Philly and was, by all accounts, a stand-up guy. I knew Mikey because he was the older brother of a girl in my third-grade class. Mikey was cool—one of the punk kids in a town where being a punk kid just wasn't okay.

I'd seen him around since elementary school—on the street, at shows, or in bars—but for some reason, I could never bring myself to say, "Hey, I was in your sister's class. Just wanted to say what's up." It had been a few years since I last saw him, as far as I could remember. Maybe that's an excuse, or perhaps it's just a defense mechanism.

The day I found out about Mikey, I received excellent advice that stuck with me. It wasn't new, but it was beautiful, as it was exactly what I needed to hear at that moment:

"Everyone should know everyone else in their life better. Don't beat yourself up about it—just know it." I know I can't get to know everyone, and I shouldn't expect to. I'm sure that I walk by wonderful, caring, compassionate people on the street every day, most of whom I'll never even say hello to. But that doesn't mean we can't take the time to truly get to know the people we do have in our lives.

Still, despite all the healing and growth I had experienced, something was missing, a purpose, a way to connect these worlds that I bounced between. That's when I got back into therapy. I found an old, wizened therapist who was sharper and brighter than me—someone who could call me out on my bullshit. Frank approached therapy from the Gestalt perspective, focusing on personal responsibility and my experience in the present moment. During our time together, I learned about new therapeutic techniques like EMDR for trauma. I talked to empty chairs to work through past relationships. Frank was a force to be reckoned with.

Though I was becoming more level-headed, I remained unstable. I needed medication—that same mood stabilizer I had fought so hard against when I was eighteen would turn out to be a lifesaver. However, I wasn't ready to accept that yet. That decision would take a few more years and a few more hard times.

It bears repeating: the most challenging times in my life were in recovery, not in active addiction. Recovery doesn't bring a perfect life. It doesn't mean your marriage will last, friends will always stand by you, or loved ones will never pass away. Recovery means learning resilience. Resilience got me through those days.

According to the APA, resilience is "the process and outcome of adapting to difficult experiences, especially through mental, emotional, and behavioral flexibility." Flexibility and adjustment are key. How does grass weather the storm while trees are uprooted? By bending with the wind. Resilience often stems from trauma. The resilience of children who survive difficult childhoods is well-documented. All of us who don't break during tough times are called "resilient."

For those in addiction, it's different but similar. Addiction brings trauma, and often, we are led to addiction through trauma. Trauma surrounds every step of addiction. For those in recovery, resilience may be the only thread keeping us together. From the outside, it may look like we're just "white-knuckling," but it's something entirely different, something more profound than just holding on. Instead, it's adapting. Changing. Bending. Letting go.

I've come to this wisdom honestly. Thirty years in recovery have brought college, grad school, heart-wrenching breakups, divorce, custody battles, and the loss of more friends and family. But through it all, I kept my head above water and maintained my recovery. That was resilience.

Where does resilience come from? Is it willpower? Family? Kids? Just the desire to see another day? What allows us to stand up through the darkest days and emerge, not unscathed, but sometimes stronger than we ever expected? For me, it's always been that faint yet stubborn voice saying, "Not today." Today is not the day to choose death, more loss, or suffering. You fall, and you get back up again. Someone is waiting for you on the other side of the struggle, maybe someone you know, someone you've yet to meet, or perhaps your future self—hoping you make it through.

I still look for and find that quiet voice in moments of tranquil meditation. With every breath, itch, or urge to move, I train my mind to let go. In this moment, everything changes and passes. Storms pass, and the wind calms again. Breathing in and out, letting go of pain, we return to the present. This simple process allows us to build resilience and the strength to adapt to life's challenges.

Most of my life has centered on suffering and on seeking relief from it. It's been years of exploring texts, religions, philosophies, and meditation practices until I finally found something that offered me hope and clarity. The resilience that meditation brings to life isn't just in moments of quiet reflection but also in moments of conflict. In times of overwhelming adversity, resilience can change our world—if we allow it. In every moment, whether filled with pain, grief, confusion, or anger, we continue to breathe. Through that breath, we find our grounding, our voice, and our resilience.

Addiction is suffering, a craving for things to be different. It's part of the human condition—the urge to distract ourselves, adjusting to external things, hoping to find happiness. We're surrounded by promises: "Look younger! Buy this car! Eat this food! Live longer!" We've been fed this tale for centuries; early storytellers spun tales of peasants marrying Prince Charming. Almost as if it's human nature, we seek out something better, newer, and different.

Instead, why not take a moment to look around and appreciate what's here? Every experience, every moment, has led to now. People strive for perfection in their homes, cars, and lives, rather than recognizing that what they have is already enough.

Just being alive is enough.

Recovery opens endless opportunities through positive, active steps to improve our lives. We plan and search for happiness—but why not find it here and now? Next time you're with someone you're attracted to, pay attention—not only to them but to what's happening within you. Notice their smile, their body language, and the look in their eyes rather than rehearsing a response. The same applies to someone you dislike. Are you focused on how they've wronged you, or can you see them as another person who, like you, simply wishes to be happy?

Too much of this life is spent on autopilot. Slow down and notice your breath, the feeling of being alive. From the time you wake, feel what it's like to have a body—to walk, eat, and breathe. Recovery has never been about achieving perfection; it's about resilience and choosing to live fully despite the setbacks. In a world obsessed with wanting more, it's easy to forget that just being alive is enough. Each breath is a reminder of our strength and a testament to the power of recovery.

Douglas Achtert, MSS, LCSW

Douglas Achtert, licensed clinical social worker, mental health therapist, meditation teacher, and writer, has been a devoted advocate for mental wellness for fourteen years. They earned their Master of Social Work degree from Bryn Mawr College in 2011.

In their work, Douglas is recognized as a relaxed, supportive, and honest partner in growth. As an empowered meditation teacher in the Theravadan tradition, they incorporate mindfulness-based cognitive therapy into their practice, utilizing the mind-body connection and cultivating awareness to carefully support clients. Through this approach, Douglas has helped many individuals grow, overcome challenges, and achieve goals across all aspects of life.

With over thirty years of recovery, Douglas brings a wealth of personal experience and compassion to their work. They live in a Philadelphia suburb with their wife, daughter, son, and dog, Willow.

"The past is over: Forgiveness means giving up all hope of a better past." –Jack Kornfield

Email: douglas.achtert@gmail.com
Instagram: @douglas.achtert

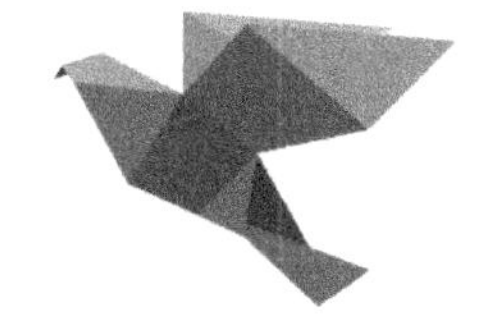

CHAPTER 12

Beyond 10,000 Days
Michael J. Rounds, B.A., L.A.C.

Ralph Waldo Emerson once said, "The only person that you are destined to become is the person that you decide to be". I am an individual who is in long-term recovery. I began my journey on January 1, 1992. I had been doing the same thing I had always done, which was sitting on a barstool drinking until I was intoxicated yet again. On May 19, 2019, I reached a substantial milestone in my recovery efforts. I celebrated 10,000 consecutive days of sustained recovery.

I started drinking when I was eighteen years old and fresh out of high school. I joined the Army in the spring of 1987 and was stationed at Fort Sill, Oklahoma. Upon completing basic training, I went with several other members of my unit to Lawton, Oklahoma, and walked into a local bar. I initially was not going to drink as I was underage at the time. However, the bartender informed me, "If I was old enough to serve my country, then I was old enough to have a drink."

I was discharged from the Army later that year due to an unknown medical condition. When I got home, I brought with me a newfound taste for alcohol, and I had to have it. I initially started drinking beer with some individuals I went to high school with. However, this soon turned into drinking a variety of alcoholic drinks. In other words, if the drink had existed at the time, I would have drunk it, including homemade moonshine. I thought, since I had served in the military, I was brave enough to continue down that path. This continued for the next five years until that fateful night on which alcohol nearly cost me my life. It is often stated that the alcoholic can remember his last drink, and this is where my journey in recovery begins.

I remember the first day of my road to recovery, and I also remember my last day of active addiction. I decided to go out with several of my friends to a local hotel to party for New Year's Eve. We had gotten to the hotel early that day and started drinking in the room since the bar did not open for a few hours. I had started drinking a few beers, and when the hotel opened, we went to the bar for the party. I started that night by drinking a couple of shots of tequila. This led to a couple more beers before midnight. When midnight came, I had a glass of champagne to ring in the New Year. After that, I had two more shots of tequila. By this time, I was pretty intoxicated. It was at this time that an individual whom I did not know had approached me and offered me the last alcoholic drink that I would consume. It was called a Flaming Dr. Pepper, which consisted of a shot of rum and half a glass of beer.

You lit the shot glass of rum on fire, dropped it in the beer, and slammed it back as you would a shot. When I drank this, I was so intoxicated that I could not walk back to my hotel room, and the bartender had to call an ambulance to take me to the hospital. While at the hospital, the medical staff had to pump my stomach to get rid of the toxins, and I was admitted to the hospital for observation. Several hours later, the doctor came to my room and had told me that due to the amount of alcohol that I had consumed, my weight at the time which was 135 pounds and not eating hardly anything before drinking, I had been on the verge of alcohol poisoning and that I had a blood alcohol content of 0.33, which was nearly 4 times the current legal limit in the state of Indiana of .08. My mother picked me up from the hospital. She drove me back to the hotel to retrieve my car. All I could do was look at the hotel and wonder if any of the guys I was drinking with had any concerns at all about my well-being. Since I had the worst hangover of my life, I drove home in silence, and all I wanted to do was crawl into my bed at my sister's house. It was a short time after I had crawled into bed that my brother-in-law at the time came knocking on my door. He was telling me to get up and get ready because he wanted me to work. I tried to tell him I was hungover and had a terrible headache, but he did not want to hear any of my excuses. He simply said to me that since I was staying at his house basically rent-free, I could get up and work and pull my share of the load. He also told me that if I was strong enough to go and party all night, then I was strong enough to get up and work.

It was while I was working that I had to decide whether I wanted to continue this lifestyle. With each hole that I had dug, the worse I felt. I knew that if I continued down this path of addiction that I had been on for the past five years, I would keep getting the same results. This gave me time to reflect on the choices I had made in my life and on how I never wanted to feel this way again. I had to look at where my life choices had taken me, and I knew that my addiction was taking me further than I ever wanted to go, making me do the things that I would have never done sober, and finally making me the person I never wanted to become. As I was digging each hole, and there were 50 of them to dig over the course of the few days, before I had to go back to work, all I could think of was how I did not want to continue to feel this way, and I had to do something about it.

People on the path to recovery often have difficulty seeing what is right in front of them. The path involves clearing the obstacles and building bridges over pitfalls. It means telling those in active addiction that you no longer want any part of the lifestyle of addiction. Only then will the path become clearer. Even though you cannot always see the path ahead, I can assure you the work is worth the reward. Remember, the only time success comes before work is in the dictionary.

Over the years that I have been in recovery, I can say my sobriety has been tested to the max. The hardest points in my sobriety were when my grandmother and my mother passed away. However, when I had lost my daughter to suicide, this nearly broke my will to maintain my sobriety.

I was twenty-six years into my recovery when I wanted to throw everything away. On August 20, 2018, I lost my fifteen-year-old daughter, Kayla, to the tragedy of suicide. I had just gotten home from working a shift at my job when one of my other children came and told me my wife was waiting for an ambulance. I immediately went into panic mode, ran into the house, and started screaming for my wife. She let me know she was upstairs, and I ran into my daughter's room only to see my wife giving my daughter CPR. When I asked her what had happened, my wife told me our daughter had hung herself. I kept screaming at her to wake up. I was pleading and begging God not to take her from us. When the ambulance arrived, the paramedics came and took over, trying to save her life.

I have been around dying people before, so I knew the signs. When I got into my daughter's bedroom, I saw that her face was ashen, and she had lost control of her bodily functions. The paramedics had brought her downstairs and were getting ready to load her in the ambulance, and all I could do was ask if she was still alive, and they told me they were doing all they could to save her. I think they did this now to give us hope, even though I think she was already gone. I was angry, mostly at myself for not protecting her. Shortly after, at the hospital, the medical staff told me she had passed away. I wanted to grab a couple of bottles and get smashed. I did not care what happened to me.

If I had been within the grasp of alcohol on this night, I think there would have been a strong possibility I would have given in to my demons. How was I able to keep from going back and using alcohol? I will tell you this was my greatest battle to date.

I had to rely on every skill I had as an individual in recovery and as a counselor. I knew I could not isolate myself and had to let everyone know not to allow me to be myself. As an individual who knows how easy it would be to give in to my addiction, I knew what would happen if I had been left to my own devices.

Over the past 33-plus years, my life has taken many twists and turns. I have had good days, bad days, and days when I wanted to throw everything away. Each time this occurred, I had to slow down and learn how to redirect my focus to reset my emotional thought patterns and not allow myself to fall into a negative, addictive thinking pattern. I simply had to breathe.

Understanding the benefits of breathing to help you manage your recovery and learning some breathing exercises can help you get through the tough days. It may seem too simple a solution for seemingly insurmountable problems, but, in fact, it is often one of the best things you can do to calm yourself down and regain a sense of clarity.

The thing I will tell you is there is nothing, and I do mean nothing, that will take the pain away. Yes, alcohol and drugs will numb the body, but the pain will come roaring back with a vengeance, and you will only want more and more.

I could not allow myself to dwell on the tragedy of losing my daughter. Each morning, I get up and remind myself, just for today I will not use, and I am stronger than the drink. Each evening, I thank God for allowing me to get through another day. It does not matter how many days you have in recovery; you must do this no matter what. Every day, we must be prepared for the fight of our lives and wear all our battle gear.

One thing my grandmother always told me was that Satan does not kick a dead horse. In other words, if you are in the depths of your addiction and are using, then there is no need for the addictive traits, thoughts, and urges to come after you because it already has you in its grasp.

This inspired me to become an addiction counselor in 2006. Each day, I remind myself why I do my job. I do not do it for the paycheck or to take care of myself financially. I get up and do this because I can make a difference in the life of an individual who still suffers, no matter what their drug of choice is. I get excited when I speak to a former client who has maintained his sobriety, and they are living a good life, knowing I had a small part in their ability to help them on the road to recovery.

Does that mean everyone I help will make it? No, but I do know that if they come back to me as a client, it is up to both of us to figure out what we did wrong the first time. Over the years, I have had several clients return to the system for the second or even third time. When an individual has sustained long-term recovery, sometimes they feel they have earned the right to drink and feel they can handle anything life will throw at them. Each time they come back, I do not chastise them for doing wrong but help them fix the issue.

One of the main things an individual in recovery must remember is to focus on what they have accomplished as well as what could have been taken away. When I had thoughts of wanting to drink, I had to remember what it was like before my recovery began. I had to remember that my drinking could have cost me my life.

Individuals in recovery must remember what it was like when they were at the worst point of their addiction. They need to focus on where they are currently in their recovery process. It is better than active addiction.

There will always be times when issues arise at work, in a relationship, or in life. However, none of this is ever worse than the nightmare of just going through life in a zombie-like state of active addiction.

I have often told others who are learning to live a new way of life that recovery is a process of training and preparation, much like getting ready for release from prison. It requires structure, awareness, and daily effort. One way I describe this process is through the **F.I.G.H.T.** framework.

F — Face the addiction

Be willing to face addiction honestly and directly, without minimizing or avoiding it. This means acknowledging its impact and accepting responsibility for change.

I — Identify risks and triggers

Identify patterns, thoughts, emotions, people, and situations that increase vulnerability to relapse. Greater awareness creates more opportunity for choice.

G — Gather tools and support

Gather the tools needed to support recovery, including coping strategies, therapy, peer support, routines, and accountability.

H — Hone skills daily

Hone recovery skills through consistent practice, reflection, and learning. Change strengthens through repetition, not perfection.

T — Take action

Take intentional, values-driven action even when it is uncomfortable. Recovery is built through daily choices, not motivation alone.

It is also important to remember that not everyone will support your recovery. Some people remain actively using and may not care that you are trying to rebuild your life. Their focus may be on pulling you back into familiar patterns and old darkness. Protecting your progress and staying committed to your path is an essential part of long-term recovery.

This is where you must be willing to train for your fight. You must be willing to get up each morning and be ready to start training. It does not matter if you do not feel like training or think you do not need to train, since you are having a great day. It is at this point and time in your life that you must be willing to work much harder than you have before, because your addiction is doing push-ups every day and is prepared for the fight against you. Working in a correctional facility, I see individuals who believe they can stand on their own and do not need to be prepared for the fight of their lives. I have seen addiction take men who had a lot going for them and knock them down, and unfortunately, spend the majority of their lives incarcerated, or worse yet, lose their lives to addiction by thinking that they could do it one more time and not be hurt. I want you to remember, it is not a matter of how many times life and addiction have knocked you down to your breaking point; what matters is the willingness to get back up, dust yourself off, and not give up and give in. I want you to know that if you are willing to fight, the better your chances are of continuing to be successful, not only in recovery but also in your life.

One of the things an individual in recovery must learn is that there are no shortcuts when it comes to changing from active addiction to being in recovery. There is no magic potion for them to become free from their addictive traits suddenly. Over the past thirty-three years, it wasn't some hocus pocus, and suddenly, I had no desire to stop using. It was a lot of blood, sweat, and tears, along with the desire to want something different in my life. The thing is, for me to be able to live a new life in recovery, I was going to have to change everything about what I had been doing during my years of active addiction.

I am telling you that you must maintain complete abstinence from using any form of alcohol or drug. I am encouraging you to keep in mind that grief puts you at a higher risk for developing a problem with alcohol or drugs, so it is imperative to seek self-awareness of the things around you. There are some things you can do to make sure your abstinence is under control, and you aren't using to self-medicate or "cope" with your grief, and to assess whether you need some changes to your behaviors or professional help. Is this something that can be accomplished by someone who is just getting started on their journey? Yes, it is possible. Has it been an easy journey thus far? Absolutely not!! I have had to work hard to get to this point in my life. I want to continue living a life in which I can be proud to say I have been in long-term recovery for over 33 years, and I have much more to go before I will ever be finished, which will be the rest of my life.

On my very worst day in recovery, I still feel a million times better than I ever did when I was drinking. I thought when I put down the beer or the whiskey, my life would be over, I would be <u>boring</u>, and everyone would think I was crazy. But when I threw away the last bottle, this is when my life really began. Now I can be the man and the father I always wanted to be. I may not be perfect, or anywhere close, but I am doing my best. Some days are still hard, but I know every time I choose to deal with my life head-on instead of numbing out the difficulties with a can or a bottle, the road gets more beautiful. It may not be easy, but it is always worth it.

Taking Recovery One Day at a Time!

Michael J. Rounds

Michael Rounds, B.A., L.A.C., is an addiction recovery specialist and works as a contractor for the Indiana Department of Correction. Mr. Rounds is an individual in long-term recovery with over 30 years of sobriety.

Michael was a speaker at the Institute of Alcohol and Drug Studies conference at the University of Southern Indiana in 2021 and the Be the Light Suicide Awareness Walk in Green Bay in 2022, where he spoke about trauma and recovery after losing his fifteen-year-old daughter to suicide in 2018.

Michael is the author of <u>"10,000 Days Sober- My 27-plus-year journey in long-term recovery".</u> He also contributed as a blogger for *Psychology Today* and *Recovery Today* Magazine.

<u>10,000 Days Sober: My 27-plus-year journey in long-term recovery</u>
<u>Rounds Article: 10,000 Days Sober: Pages 48-50</u>

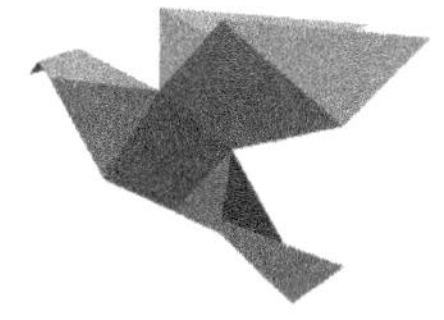

CHAPTER 13

The Multiple Tries to Recovery
Until I got on the Path I Needed

Anthony Locascio

My story of recovery started in October 1994, when I was arrested in school for smoking pot. As I was taken out of the school in handcuffs, at lunchtime, I realized that I might have a problem. The first rehab that I went to, immediately after this, was short-lived, and I was getting high again after being discharged from that facility. From October 1994 to June 1995, I used drugs almost every day, obsessing from the time that I woke up till the time I went to sleep on how I would get more drugs, what I would have to do to get more, and how I could make it all happen. I did not use drugs that I was physically dependent on, so I was not sick in the morning, but I was obsessed as soon as I opened my eyes.

My recovery story began when I was sixteen. I had reached the end of my road and entered my third inpatient drug rehabilitation facility in June 1995. I remember smelling and being slightly embarrassed. I remember feeling wrung out; I couldn't keep going on the way I was going. I was constantly tired, exhausted, and just spent from the drugs, the obsession with drugs, and the mental anguish that I was living through. I knew I needed to stop since I had been abusing drugs, which I had been doing since I was 11, but I had no idea how. My background with my parents led me to think these actions of addiction were normal. From as early as

I can remember, I endured adverse childhood experiences, including corporal punishment, verbal abuse, and emotional neglect from my parents. They believed that being a latchkey kid was normal, allowing me to fend for myself while they worked long hours.

Both of my parents were small business owners. My mother owned a business my grandfather started in the 1920s, dedicating six days a week to it until she retired in 2019. Throughout my childhood and teenage years, my dad was a small business owner who worked constantly. My mother had four children from her first marriage, but there is a generational gap between my older siblings and me. My oldest niece was the same age as my younger sister, so by the time I was a teenager, my older siblings were out of the house and no longer involved in my life.

My mother would start drinking wine and beer at her office as soon as the clock struck 6 p.m., so I knew not to engage her in conversation when she came home, as she would not remember it the next morning. I saw my father less frequently, but when I did, he was usually drinking heavily, though he seemed to retain his memory in the morning. One of my earliest memories is of him punching a wall, leaving a fist-sized hole. It was not surprising when he began hitting me to get me to comply with his wishes.

My parents had a unique way of showing me love through gifts, but they never made time or space for me to approach them with questions or seek guidance. I found comfort in drinking wine from the family room bar, which was unlocked and readily available. No one seemed to notice or care that I was sneaking sips.

My parents had another child, my sister, who was five and a half years younger than me; she was in diapers when a neighborhood male babysitter sexually assaulted her. I am not sure how old I was at the time; I do not have clear memories of the incident, and I did not remember it until I was in 7th grade in English class. It was during a fellow student's presentation on sexual assault/traumatic memories that the memories from my sister's assault came flooding back. Even then, my memory of the event remained unclear. I did not know how to handle this sudden rush of recollection, and I did not feel safe talking to my parents about it. However, I was familiar with how my parents coped with their own stressors, so I followed suit. If I drank, everything would be okay, and as long as I kept working or stayed distracted, I'd manage- at least on the surface.

So, I did what my parents taught me: I turned to drugs and, at times, alcohol. Since I was underage, drugs were easier to get than alcohol. I remember my first time getting high; it was like running through a field, feeling completely carefree, convinced everything would be okay. I cherished that feeling and desperately wanted to find it again. But no matter how many drugs I used, I could never fully recapture that initial feeling again.

In October 1994, when I was fifteen, I was sent away to my first inpatient drug and alcohol treatment facility, where I stayed for about a week. However, I did not stay clean or sober after leaving. I was put into an intensive outpatient program (IOP) in Chester, PA, which required me to attend group psychotherapy three days a week after school. My dad drove me to these sessions and was somewhat supportive of my efforts to find and achieve sobriety; however, I wasn't ready for that change and continued down the path I was on.

From October 1994 to June 1995, the only time that I was not high was during the week that I spent in that inpatient facility. I attended the IOP because my parents made me, but my behavior did not change. Eventually, the program decided I needed a higher level of care and referred me to a partial hospitalization program (PHP). This program ran from 9 a.m. to 5 p.m., four days a week. I am not sure how long I stayed in PHP, but I know I did not stop getting high while I was in that program.

I felt utterly trapped by the drugs. I craved the euphoria I had experienced when I first used it, but it was elusive. Each morning, when I would open my eyes, my first thought would be that I was not high yet—and that I needed to find a way to get high for the day. I was stuck in a vicious cycle: the drugs weren't making me feel good anymore, and I could not bear the memories of all the traumatic incidents. Before I knew it, I began using the drugs to make the memories disappear and to dull the pain.

All of this came crashing down in June 1995. The drugs could no longer keep the memories repressed, and at that point in my life, I did not have the tools or coping skills to process them. That is when I decided to walk down the train tracks, hoping a train would run me over and end it all. At the last moment, I had the presence of mind to stumble off the train tracks into the bushes just before the train sped past. When I got off the train tracks, I knew what was waiting for me if I continued to use and experiment with my addiction. It was then that I realized I needed help.

I reached out to a family friend, who found me a spot in a rehab facility that agreed to take me for the summer of 1995.

However, before I entered that rehab, I had a going-away party thrown by the friends that I had made during my addiction. Of the eight people who were at that party, five are no longer alive, lost to drugs or a life of crime related to drugs. I think a few of them went on to use opioids, which were not widely available in the mid-90s, as they would become available in the following years.

I remember going into the rehab and being embarrassed that I smelled poorly, but the intake staff comforted me, stating it was normal. After a few days, I wanted to leave, but then there was a moment of clarity when two people from Narcotics Anonymous (NA) came into the rehab to speak to us. I felt I could relate to the speakers in a way I hadn't before. They talked the way I spoke; they said a lot of the things I felt, and they had used similar drugs that I had. However, they also talked about a new way of life, a path that I did not fully understand at the time. Their words sparked a sense of hope that I had never experienced before.

Before meeting them, I did not think change was possible for me. I was not trying to do anything different in the rehab—I was just passing the time, as I had done in the previous treatments. However, after they visited, it felt like they touched something in my spirit, and I found the motivation to do things I had envisioned for myself, but I did not have the strength or the commitment to do them. I volunteered for assignments (e.g., cooking meals for others and leading community meetings) in rehab until I became the "mayor" of the rehab and actively participated in group counseling sessions. I also began listening and taking suggestions from the counselors and my peers. I even started doing Hayon One, a kata from Kempo Karate, in the rehab's front yard. Although I had started a martial arts journey before going into rehab, I had not devoted myself to it the way that I wanted.

The rehab awakened in me a desire for self-improvement and ultimately set me on a path towards enlightenment. I found a Buddhist Sanga that welcomed me and taught me how to meditate in the Za-Zen tradition. Walking towards a path of enlightenment is a lifelong journey. I am not a perfect Buddhist or meditator, but I find that emotional stability and peace of mind are possible through mindful activities.

Before my rehab, I carried tremendous guilt because I thought I should have been able to protect my sister. After I remembered what had happened to her, I could not process those memories on my own. I needed tools to integrate those terrible memories so I could function in society. Therapy and the twelve-step process became another space where I could begin processing and healing.

In September 1995, when I was released from rehab—shortly before high school started—I attended my first NA meeting. I quickly fell into a rhythm with meetings, dedicating myself to attending one a day for at least the first 90 days. This soon turned into a daily commitment for my first two years of sobriety. In NA, I found a home group, a sponsor, service commitments, and people who were like me—people who experienced the darkness of addiction but had come out the other side and managed to do something different with their lives. A sponsor is a person who is supposed to guide you through the twelve steps, but they can be many more things than this. My first sponsor helped to shape and guide me toward finding a passion for recovery that I had not known previously. They also guided me through the first five steps of NA. After sharing my searching and fearless moral inventory (also known as the fourth step) with this man, we both moved on to another sponsor.

My second sponsor is a man of faith and purpose and has been clean and sober for as long as I have been alive! I went to him because he has great wisdom and humility, and I sought to incorporate both traits into my daily life. He guided me through the rest of the steps and gave me a great understanding and respect for service work in NA. He also became my moral compass and a guide in my faith; if I struggled with recovery (or in life), I knew I could turn to him, and he would help me through it. He also showed me that perfection is not a goal; we would joke about how he would go to the casino to pull the "one arm bandit" and how he knew it was silly, but would still do it. It helped me see that I did not need to be perfect in all my affairs and that it is okay to struggle.

My sponsor's guidance also helped me to learn how to sponsor others. I have been a sponsor many times over the years in recovery and have had the privilege of watching people come into a twelve-step fellowship, take their first steps, learn how to live a different way, and flourish in that new way of life. I have also watched many people come into recovery, not fully grasp or understand the recovery process, and ultimately die of their addiction. This was especially true in 2016, which was a challenging year for my friend group, as eight people that I was close with died of an overdose. I could grieve those who did not find their new way of life and inspire growth and change in others that came along in the years since. Being a sponsor for people is a privilege and an honor, and I do my best to be the best sponsor that I can be.

In addition to my twelve-step recovery, I began attending a Kempo Karate studio a few nights a week and working out in a gym a few days before or after school. My martial arts journey started with Kempo but moved on to Chinese Kung Fu, Taekwondo, boxing, kickboxing, and, most recently, action karate. I have been in martial arts for over twenty-five years. The desire to find some resolution and healing from the trauma that I experienced as a child fueled this movement towards self-improvement. Recovery, for me, is a mind-body-physical change. Addiction is a mind, body, and physical disease, so recovery should match that. Sometimes physical recovery means going to the doctor to make sure everything is okay, but other times it can involve physical fitness. At first, for me, it was simply going to the local YMCA to play basketball and mess around with the weights. As I continued in recovery, I became an avid runner, going so far as to finish a marathon in 2012, running the Broad Street Run twelve times, and running a 5k in 19:36. I also believe that fitness helps me to process some of the stress, anxiety, and desire to pick up drugs and alcohol again.

In my progress, I found a community that sustained my recovery and provided me with a model of service to others. Over the years, I volunteered for many hours at NA, helping establish several local meetings and serving in regional and national leadership positions.

During this time, I developed the personal values of honesty, humility, and accountability. Most germane to my current professional pursuit, I developed compassion for others and a strong passion for improving the lives of those affected by addiction.

After spending the summer of 1995 in rehab, I felt reasonably confident in my ability to maintain my recovery. However, academics were another story. I was a mess. During my first two years of high school, my GPA was below 1.0, and I did not attend regularly. When I did go, I would get high before and after school. I got into a few fights and was eventually asked not to come back to my high school. Thankfully, my parents had an apartment in another school district, and I was able to attend a different school while living with one of my half-brothers (my mother had four kids from a previous relationship, and my sister and I are from my parents).

For a while, I struggled to gain any traction in my education. I graduated from high school a year later than I was supposed to, in 1998, and did not go to college immediately afterward. I was not ready for the academic challenges that college brought. It took a few years and several attempts at community college before I found my academic footing.

It wasn't until I took a few psychopharmacology classes that I realized my brain needed time to heal and adjust to life without chemicals. By 2002, I saw improvement and began building academic success. In 2003, I transferred to the University of Pennsylvania and graduated in 2007.

After earning a BA degree from the University of Pennsylvania, I spent several years working in information technology. However, when I began a part-time job as a personal trainer, I realized I wanted to combine my passion for helping others in the NA community with my professional career. This realization led me to the Counseling Psychology Master's Program at Immaculata University in Pennsylvania.

I found the graduate-level courses very stimulating and rewarding, and I became a member of the Chi Sigma Iota Counseling Honor Society, serving as the president of the Beta Mu Chapter in my final year.

Currently, I am a licensed professional counselor (LPC) in Pennsylvania, Arizona, and West Virginia, and a certified advanced alcohol and drug counselor (CAADC) since 2021. My professional career has included working with children with behavior disorders and autism, as well as adults who are suffering from addiction. Additionally, from 2015 to 2021, I worked as a detox counselor at the Livengrin Foundation, a drug and alcohol inpatient facility. This allowed me to work just outside Philadelphia, where I have encountered many adults who are greatly afflicted by the opioid crisis and have been able to guide some of them to recovery.

 However, in 2021, I had to stop working at Livengrin when I started my doctorate at Holy Family University. Though bittersweet, stepping away from the job at the rehab center allowed me to focus on advancing my education while continuing to help others. In fact, I also started my counseling business in 2021 as part of a natural evolution of my career. Currently, I am on track to graduate with my doctorate in psychology in 2026.

During my doctoral training, I learned about the prescribing movement for psychologists and immediately recognized it as a natural fit for me. As a result, in 2023, I started my master's in clinical psychopharmacology, and I will complete that coursework by 2025. I continue to use my personal background and professional training to help as many people as I can.

Anthony Locascio

I am from Philadelphia, PA, and still live here today. Currently, I am a PsyD student at Holy Family University and working on a Master's in Clinical Psychopharmacology at the Chicago School for Professional Psychology. I also run my own private practice as a licensed professional counselor (LPC), which you can see at my website:

www.locwellness.com.

In my limited free time, I enjoy spending time with my girlfriend, Liz, our large dog, Cyrus, and my niece, Anna. I also enjoy a good motorcycle ride to the gym of my choice.

INTRODUCTION TO THE SECOND SECTION OF THE BOOK

The first section of this book shares the personal journeys of thirteen people in recovery—showing that change is possible, even when it feels out of reach. Their experiences provide inspiration, insight, and reveal grief and grace, relapses and rebounds, as well as the quiet daily choices that build a different life.

The second section shifts from story to how. It's designed for three readers: (1) someone currently struggling, (2) someone active in recovery, and (3) someone who loves a person with an addiction. Addiction doesn't live in isolation; it ripples through families, classrooms, workplaces, and neighborhoods. So, the guidance here is practical, person-centered, and adaptable.

I have sat in every chair of this conversation- clinician, educator, someone who loves someone with an addiction, someone struggling with their addiction, and someone who now has over 16 years of continued recovery from drugs and alcohol. You will not find a single "right way" in these pages. You will discover multiple pathways, including mutual help, therapy, faith-based support, skills training, harm reduction, and community engagement. Each chapter ends with clear next steps and an invitation to add your own wisdom.

Why This Section Matters

Recovery is not a one-size-fits-all process. While common themes and evidence-based approaches can be helpful, every journey is deeply personal and unique. This part of the book aims to guide different perspectives:

For Those Struggling with Addiction – If you find yourself caught in the cycle of addiction, you are not alone. This section provides insight into what addiction is, why it occurs, and, most importantly, how to take the first steps toward change. Whether you are contemplating recovery or unsure whether it is possible for you, this section provides information on treatment options, therapy, NAMI (National Alliance on Mental Illness) resources, 12-step programs, and alternative support groups, as well as practical strategies to initiate the recovery process.

For Those Actively in recovery, recovery is an ongoing journey that requires continuous commitment, support, and self-discovery. This section will focus on maintaining sobriety, navigating challenges such as cravings and setbacks, building a strong support network, and developing a fulfilling life beyond addiction. It will also explore strategies for long-term personal growth, purpose, and well-being.

For Loved Ones of Those Struggling with Addiction – Addiction is often called a family disease because it deeply affects those around the individual who is struggling. If you are a parent, spouse, sibling, or friend of someone with an addiction, this section will offer guidance on how to support them while maintaining your own well-being. Topics include setting healthy boundaries, understanding addiction and recovery, self-care, and available resources for family members.

The Importance of a Person-Centered Approach

This book does not advocate a single "right way" to recover. Instead, it embraces a person-centered approach—recognizing that everyone's recovery process is unique. We will highlight multiple pathways to healing, including therapy and peer support, as well as faith-based recovery and harm reduction approaches. By incorporating real-life experiences, research-based strategies, and actionable resources, we aim to equip you with the knowledge and support you need for your specific situation.

How to Use This Section

Each chapter is designed to be both informative and practical. Throughout these pages, you will find:

- Evidence-based insights into addiction, recovery, and behavioral health.

- Resources include national helplines, organizations like NAMI, and online support communities.

- Personal reflections and prompts to help you apply what you learn.

- Actionable steps to support your next move, whether that is seeking help, strengthening your recovery, or helping a loved one.

A Final Note

No matter where you are on this journey, whether at the beginning, in the middle, or supporting someone else, know that recovery is possible. Hope is real. Change is within reach. You are not alone. This section is designed to offer guidance, compassion, and the tools to help you take the next step towards healing and growth.

Let's begin.

FOR SOMEONE WHO IS STRUGGLING WITH ADDICTION

You Are Not Alone

Therapy: A Safe Place to Heal

Therapy can be a game-changer in the recovery process. When you're feeling lost, overwhelmed, or unsure of where to start, a good therapist can help you slow down, cultivate curiosity, and begin the deep work of healing. They won't judge you for your past or your struggles. Instead, they'll help you better understand yourself, your addiction, your emotions, your patterns, and the pain that may lie beneath it all.

One of the most powerful aspects of therapy is that it provides a space for you to be seen and heard, sometimes for the first time in a long time. Therapies like cognitive behavioral therapy (CBT) and dialectical behavior therapy (DBT) are especially effective for people in recovery. CBT teaches you to identify and challenge harmful thoughts and beliefs, while DBT helps build emotional regulation, mindfulness, and distress tolerance. Both approaches can empower you to respond to life rather than react—and that can make a significant difference.

Other modalities like EMDR (used for trauma), motivational interviewing (used to build readiness for change), and Parts Work/Internal Family Systems (IFS) can also be deeply transformative. The most important part is finding a therapist who makes you feel safe, seen, and supported.

If you're unsure where to begin, organizations like NAMI (National Alliance on Mental Illness) can help connect you to qualified therapists, often based on your needs, finances, or identity. Many therapists now offer telehealth options, making it easier than ever to access support—regardless of whether you live in a rural area, work long hours, or struggle with transportation.

You can also explore therapist directories like:

- **Psychology Today** – Search by insurance, specialty, and location.

- **Therapy for Black Girls / Therapy for Black Men**

- **Inclusive Therapists** – A directory centering BIPOC, LGBTQ+, and neurodivergent communities.

- **Open Path Collective** – Low-cost therapy options on a sliding scale.

12-Step and Peer Support Groups: Strength in Community

Millions of people have found lasting recovery through 12-step programs like Alcoholics Anonymous (AA), Narcotics Anonymous (NA), Al-Anon, and others. These meetings provide more than just a seat in a circle—they offer a structured, judgment-free community where you can speak openly about your struggles, celebrate your wins, and feel truly seen by others who've walked a similar road.

12-step programs follow guiding principles like honesty, humility, service, and accountability. While they are not religious, they do emphasize a connection to a "Higher Power"—something greater than yourself that can support your healing. For many, that idea brings comfort, surrender, and strength. For others, it may feel unfamiliar or even uncomfortable, and that's okay.

As one member shared, *"When I walked into my first meeting, I was terrified. But someone greeted me, gave me a seat, and told me, 'Keep coming back.' That's what I did, and my life has changed."*

If the spiritual framework of the 12-steps doesn't resonate with you, there are powerful **alternatives** that may be a better fit:

SMART Recovery

- (Self-Management and Recovery Training) It is a science-based, self-empowering program that focuses on cognitive and behavioral tools to help individuals maintain their sobriety. It teaches skills like managing cravings, increasing motivation, and living a balanced life.

Recovery Dharma

- Grounded in Buddhist principles, Recovery Dharma is a peer-led community that uses meditation, self-inquiry, and mindfulness to break the cycle of suffering and addiction.

LifeRing Secular Recovery

- A non-religious, self-help support group for people who want to develop their own personalized recovery plan. The focus is on strengthening the "sober self" and encouraging mutual respect and support.

Celebrate Recovery

- A Christian-based 12-step program that integrates faith with healing and is often offered in churches.

Women for Sobriety

- A group designed specifically for women, emphasizing empowerment, self-worth, and emotional growth in recovery.

The Phoenix

- A sober active community that combines fitness, wellness, and social connection. Whether it's yoga, climbing, or CrossFit, all events are free for those with 48 hours of sobriety.

Each of these groups is built around the same powerful truth: **You are not alone.** Peer support gives you the chance to listen, be heard, learn, and grow in the company of others who understand addiction firsthand.

Whether it's a large in-person meeting, a small virtual circle, or a message board in an app, the key is to find a community where you feel safe, understood, and encouraged.

Recovery doesn't require perfection, just asks for honesty and connection. Whether you're speaking or just listening, showing up is enough.

If you're reading this, some of you still believe change is possible. That's enough to start. You don't need to be perfect, fearless, or ready for forever, just need to be ready for today.

For the next 24 hours:

- Tell one safe person: "I'm not okay, and I need help."

- Pick one doorway: call a treatment line, text a crisis line, attend a meeting (online or in-person), or schedule a therapist intake appointment. Any door that leads you towards people will take you away from loneliness and isolation.

- Set a "danger hour" plan: When cravings hit, I will (1) call/text___________, (2) take a cold shower or step outside for 10 minutes, (3) eat something, (4) start a 20-minute timer before any decision. You can add the main goal of making healthier decisions to this list, which will move you towards recovery.

- Make your space safer: delete phone numbers, discard what no longer serves a purpose, and adjust your route if certain places draw you in.

- If alcohol/benzos/opioids are involved: ask a medical professional about safe detox (safety first).

Understanding Addiction: Quick and Honest

This isn't a willpower problem. Addiction alters the reward, stress, and decision-making systems in the brain. That's why recovery isn't about trying harder; it's about getting help and practicing skills until your brain and life catch up. Shame doesn't help you heal; support does.

Breaking the Cycle

Noticing "I have a problem" is a beginning, not a verdict. Awareness needs a plan:

- **Write one sentence of why:** "I want to wake up proud," "I want to be there for my kids," "I am tired of living like this," or "I don't want to die." Whatever one sentence resonates with you, write it down; this could be the start you need towards recovery.

- **Name your top three triggers:** people, places, things, feelings, times.

- **Create an If/Then statement:** If it's 9 pm and I am restless, then I will call ______, walk for 10 minutes, and attend a meeting.

Finding Support: Connection Beats Isolation

You don't have to do this alone. Choose one path to start; add others as you go.

- **Therapy** can help you understand patterns, regulate emotions, and develop skills. The "right" therapist is the one you feel safe with and trust.

- **Peer Support:** Organizations such as AA/NA, SMART Recovery, Recovery Dharma, LifeRing, Celebrate Recovery, and others can help you build your sober support network. Try a few meetings before you decide what is the right fit for you.

- **Your People:** one friend, sponsor, or faith leader who will answer when you say, "I'm having a hard hour." Consistency over perfection.

A Note from My Own Journey

I'll be honest, none of these came easy to me at first. I read lists like this and thought, *"Sure, maybe for other people, but not for me."* I struggled with therapy, with meetings, even with letting people get close enough to help. What made the difference was permitting myself to try again, even when I hated it. Finding the right therapist took time, but once I did, it was like someone finally spoke my language and helped me make sense of my patterns.

Meetings were another hurdle. Early on, I sat there counting all the things I didn't like. The breakthrough came when I shifted my focus: instead of walking out with ten complaints, I made myself look for one positive thing, a phrase, a story, even just a sense of relief that I wasn't alone. That one thing became enough to keep me coming back. And just as important, I had to be intentional about the people around me. I learned the hard way that some folks, even well-meaning ones, enabled me in ways that kept me stuck. What truly helped was surrounding myself with people who were real to me, people who cared enough to tell me the truth even when I didn't want to hear it. They weren't always comfortable to be around, but they loved me enough to hold me accountable, and that's what I needed. That combination —finding a therapist I connected with, reframing how I viewed meetings, and leaning on people who wanted the best for me —changed everything. It didn't make recovery easy, but it made it possible.

What to Expect When You Seek Help

Taking the first step toward recovery can feel overwhelming. Here is what you might experience:

Fear and Uncertainty

It's normal to feel scared when you step into recovery. Fear doesn't mean you can't do it; it just means you care about what's at stake. Growth often starts on the edge of fear, but you don't have to white-knuckle through it. Here are a few ways to work with fear when it shows up:

- **Name it out loud.** Saying "I feel scared right now" takes away some of fear's power and helps you separate the feeling from who you are.

- **Shrink the timeline.** Instead of thinking, "How will I stay sober forever?" ask, "What can I do for the next hour?" or "What will help me get through today?"

- **4-7-8 breathing.** Inhale through your nose for 4 seconds, hold for 7 seconds, and slowly exhale through your mouth for 8 seconds. Repeat four cycles. This helps calm your nervous system and reduces anxiety in the moment.

- **Ground yourself with 5-4-3-2-1.** Notice five things you see, four things you feel, three things you hear, two things you smell, and one thing you taste. This pulls you out of spiraling thoughts and back into the present.

- **Borrow courage.** Fear shrinks when you don't face it alone. Call a sponsor, text a peer, or ask someone to go with you. Sometimes leaning on someone else's strength gets you through.

Fear doesn't disappear before you act. It fades because you act. Each time you move forward scared, you're proving to yourself that recovery is possible.

Physical and Emotional Withdrawal

Depending on the substance or behavior you are trying to stop, withdrawal can include both physical and psychological symptoms. These symptoms can range from mild (irritability, fatigue, or restlessness) to severe and life-threatening (such as seizures or hallucinations). Substances like alcohol, benzodiazepines, and opioids often require medical supervision to detox safely and reduce the risk of complications.

But withdrawal isn't just physical. Emotional withdrawal is just as real—and sometimes even more difficult. Feelings of depression, anxiety, hopelessness, and emotional numbness are common. You may feel like you've lost your only coping mechanism. It's essential to recognize that this phase is temporary, even when it feels unbearable.

Many people relapse during withdrawal, not just to avoid physical discomfort, but because of the emotional intensity that comes with it. Having a support system, professional help, and a plan in place can make all the difference. Withdrawal is not a sign of weakness—it's part of the healing process. You don't have to go through it alone.

Cravings and Triggers

You will face moments where the urge to use feels overwhelming. Cravings can be physical, emotional, or situational, triggered by stress, certain individuals, specific places, or particular memories. This is why having a relapse prevention plan and a strong support system is critical.

A relapse prevention plan is a personalized roadmap that helps you recognize high-risk situations and outlines how to respond without turning back to substances or behaviors. It often includes:

- Your **triggers** (people, places, feelings, or situations that put you at risk)

- **Early warning signs** of relapse (isolation, skipping meetings, "just one won't hurt" thinking)

- **Coping strategies** (calling a support person, using grounding or breathing techniques, going to a meeting, exercising, journaling)

- **Daily routines** that keep you steady (sleep, meals, self-care, check-ins)

- **Support contacts** (sponsor, therapist, friends, family)

- **Emergency steps** if cravings escalate (removing yourself from a situation, calling a crisis line, going to a meeting, or seeking professional help)

To create your plan, reflect on past relapses or close calls that you've experienced. What led up to them? What thoughts, emotions, or circumstances made using feel like an option? Write these down, then identify ways to interrupt that cycle with healthier choices. Keep your plan short, simple, and somewhere you can access quickly, like your phone, a wallet card, or taped to your fridge.

Here's an example of what a plan might look like:

My Why: "I want to wake up proud and be present for my kids."

Triggers: Friday paydays, stress at work, driving past old bars, boredom

Warning Signs: Skipping therapy, avoiding calls, replaying resentments

Coping Strategies: Call my sponsor, practice 4-7-8 breathing, 5-4-3-2-1 grounding, take a walk, attend a meeting

Daily Routine: Sleep 11–6, three meals, 20 minutes of movement, gratitude journal at night

Support System: Sponsor Mike (phone number), partner Jess (phone number), peer Sam (phone number)

Emergency Plan: Leave triggering situation, call Mike or Sam, go to the nearest meeting, call 988 if unsafe

Recommitment Statement: "I will ask for help before I pick up. One day at a time, I choose recovery."

You can find free relapse prevention templates online from organizations such as SAMHSA, NAMI, and SMART Recovery. But the most important thing is making it yours. A strong plan doesn't just focus on what not to do; it gives you clear actions to take instead.

Having a plan in place doesn't mean you'll never struggle. It means when the struggle comes, you'll already know what to do.

Hope and Breakthroughs

Though it may feel painful at first, recovery is not about pain; it is about freedom. In the early stages, it's normal to feel overwhelmed or uncertain. Letting go of something that once felt like your only escape can be daunting. But as the fog begins to lift, so does your capacity to heal and grow.

You'll begin to experience small but powerful victories: a clear mind that can focus and reflect, deeper, more authentic connections with others, and the return of something many people in recovery forget they deserve—a sense of self-worth. These moments may come quietly at first: making it through a tough day without using, laughing at something silly, sleeping through the night, or hearing yourself say "no" to an old trigger. But over time, they build into breakthroughs.

You'll begin to rediscover the parts of yourself that addiction buried—your resilience, your values, your voice. And when those moments arrive, they will remind you why you began this journey: not to be perfect, but to be free, to be present, and to be *you*.

Hope doesn't erase the struggle, but it gives it meaning. Recovery is a series of awakenings—and every step forward is proof that transformation is not only possible but already happening.

You Are Worth It

I know it is hard. I know it feels impossible. But I also know that you are capable of more than you think. You are not your addiction; you are a person who deserves peace, love, and a fulfilling life.

This journey will not be perfect. You may stumble, but stumbling is not falling. Every time you get back up, you are proving your strength. You don't have to do it all at once, just take the next step. And then the next.

Recovery is not about becoming someone new; it's about returning to yourself, your values, your voice, your hope. You are not broken. You are becoming. Keep going.

You are worth it.
Always have been.
Always will be.

FOR SOMEONE ACTIVE IN THEIR RECOVERY

You Have Come So Far—Keep Going

If you are reading this, it means you have already taken the brave steps needed to get sober and commit to recovery. That alone is incredible. Whether you are a few weeks, months, or years into this journey, I want you to take a moment to recognize how far you have come.

Recovery is not only about quitting substances—it is about building a fulfilling life beyond addiction. You are no longer just surviving; you are creating a future filled with meaning, purpose, and hope.

The Reality of Long-Term Recovery

Many people think that once the physical cravings subside, recovery gets easier. While some aspects do, other challenges emerge. Emotional triggers, relationships, and daily stress can test your commitment. But here is the good news: you are equipped to handle it.

Staying Connected to Your Support System

One of the most significant indicators of long-term recovery success is maintaining engagement with a support system. Whether it is a 12-step group like AA or NA, therapy, or organizations like NAMI, having a community that understands you is essential.

- **Meetings and Groups:** Keep attending support meetings, even when you feel strong. Remember, there is strength in numbers. Connection is what keeps recovery sustainable.

- **Therapy:** Continue therapy or counseling, especially if you are working through underlying trauma or mental health challenges.

- **Check in with Yourself:** Journaling, mindfulness, and meditation can help you stay aware of your emotions and triggers. Writing doesn't need to be long; just a few sentences each day can bring clarity. Here are some prompts you might try:

  o   What emotions did I feel most strongly today, and how did I respond to them?

  o   What was one situation that challenged my recovery, and how did I handle it?

  o   What am I grateful for right now, even if it feels small?

  o   What is one thing I can do tomorrow that supports my recovery?

Am I noticing any early warning signs, such as isolation, irritability, or negative thinking, that I need to address?

Checking in with yourself through journaling keeps you honest about where you are, helps you spot patterns before they turn into setbacks, and lets you track your progress over time.

Managing Triggers and Avoiding Complacency

As time passes, it's natural to start feeling more confident in your recovery. But addiction is a chronic condition—one that doesn't go away just because things are going well. In fact, comfort and complacency can quietly increase vulnerability to relapse. Staying aware and proactive helps protect your progress.

- **Identify potential triggers:** Triggers can be external (such as stress, conflict, or specific places or people) or internal (like boredom, shame, overconfidence, or emotional fatigue).

- *The more clearly you can name your triggers, the more power you have to prepare for them and respond instead of reacting.*

- **Examine your relapse prevention plan:** Identify your early warning signs—such as skipping meetings, isolating, minimizing urges, or feeling "numb" again—and develop action steps for when they appear. A plan isn't something you write once and tuck away. It should grow with you. Revisit and revise it often, especially after changes in your routine, relationships, or stress level.

Ask yourself:

- Are there new triggers in my life I need to add?

- Have I discovered coping tools that really work for me and should be written into my plan?

- Do the people on my support contact list still pick up the phone when I call?

Think of your plan like a living document. If it stays the same for too long, it can get stale and easy to forget. By updating it, you keep it relevant and personal to your current life. Some people review their plan weekly; others update it after a close call or a breakthrough in therapy. You might even set a monthly reminder to review it, make at least one small adjustment, and update it accordingly. The more you interact with your plan, the more natural it becomes to use it when you need it most.

Keep an emergency contact list: A sponsor, therapist, recovery peer, or trusted friend who knows your story and will pick up the phone when you call.

- *Have it written down and easily accessible. In a moment of struggle, having someone to reach out to can make all the difference.*

Schedule check-ins with yourself: Ask regularly, "How am I doing emotionally, spiritually, physically?"

- *Awareness is your first line of defense. Don't wait for a crisis to reconnect with the practices that keep you grounded.*

Celebrate progress but stay humble: Milestones are worth honoring—but recovery isn't graduation.

- *Complacency can lead to old thinking. Stay connected to your why and keep doing the work, even when it's going well.*

Building a Meaningful Life Beyond Addiction

Sobriety is about more than not using—it's about creating a life so fulfilling, you no longer feel the urge to escape from it. Recovery is not just the absence of substances; it's the *presence* of purpose, connection, and joy. It's about seeing not just who you were in addiction, but who you're becoming in healing.

This part of the journey is where you begin to rediscover what lights you up—whether it's relationships, creativity, career goals, spirituality, or simply waking up without regret. You may find meaning in giving back, helping others who are still struggling, or reconnecting with family in ways that once felt impossible.

It's also about learning how to enjoy life on life's terms. You'll face stress and loss, as everyone does—but now you have tools, community, and clarity to guide you through. As you grow, your sober life becomes richer, deeper, and more aligned with your values.

You don't have to have all the answers today. Start exploring what makes you feel *whole*, not just "clean." Recovery gives you the opportunity to rebuild—not just a life free from harm, but a life full of meaning, freedom, and peace.

Finding Purpose and Passion

Recovery doesn't just remove something from your life—it makes space to discover what really matters to you. Purpose gives direction, and passion brings energy. Together, they help transform recovery from something you have to do into a life you *want to live.*

Explore new hobbies and passions: What excites you or makes you feel alive? Maybe it's painting, writing, running, cooking, hiking, or dancing.

- *Trying something new or returning to a long-forgotten interest can reconnect you with joy, creativity, and a sense of identity.*

Give back to the recovery community: Whether it's sharing your story, sponsoring someone, or simply attending a meeting, helping others strengthens your own recovery.

- *Service fosters gratitude, accountability, and the powerful reminder that your experience can inspire someone else's hope.*

Set new personal and professional goals: Think about what you want your future to look like. That might include going back to school, applying for a job you thought was out of reach, or working toward healthier relationships.

- *Progress doesn't have to be fast; it just needs to be meaningful to you.*

Let your story become a source of strength: Everything you've survived gives you insight and empathy.

- *Your pain doesn't define you—but it can shape a purpose that helps others heal, too.*

Strengthening Relationships

Addiction often strains or severs meaningful relationships—but recovery creates space for healing, reconnection, and new beginnings. Rebuilding trust and surrounding yourself with people who uplift you is essential for long-term recovery.

Rebuild trust with loved ones: Recovery enables you to present yourself as the best version of yourself—honest, present, and dependable.

- *Rebuilding trust takes time. Let your actions speak louder than promises. Apologize when needed, listen when it's hard, and stay consistent. Trust grows one moment at a time.*

Surround yourself with positive people: Stay connected to those who support your journey and remind you of your worth.

- *You deserve relationships that make you feel safe, respected, and valued. Seek out people who celebrate your growth—not just tolerate it.*

Set healthy boundaries: Not everyone will understand or respect your recovery—and that's okay. You are allowed to protect your peace.

- *In early recovery, it's crucial to pay attention to people, places, and things that may trigger old habits or pull you off course. Boundaries aren't walls; they're bridges to a healthier you. They allow you to love others without losing yourself.*

Practice open and honest communication: Recovery thrives on authenticity. Be real about how you're feeling, what you need, and where you're still growing.

- *Vulnerability builds connection. You don't have to pretend to have it all figured out, just be willing to stay in the conversation.*

Forgive, but don't forget your growth: Some relationships may need repair, and others may need to end. That's part of healing, too.

- *Forgiveness doesn't mean ignoring harm. It means choosing peace over resentment and making room for relationships that support the person you're becoming.*

When Challenges Arise: Staying Resilient

Even in recovery, life will bring difficulties—such as financial stress, breakups, loss, disappointment, or moments of deep self-doubt. These are not signs of failure. These are the moments when your recovery is tested—and where resilience is built.

- **Reach out to your support network**: You don't have to do it alone. *Reach out before the spiral begins. Whether it's a sponsor, therapist, friend, or support group, letting someone in can shift everything. Connection is your lifeline in difficult moments.*

- **Practice self-care**: Sleep, nutrition, movement, and emotional wellness are not luxuries—they're necessities. *Self-care in hard times doesn't have to be perfect. Even small acts, such as eating a meal, taking a walk, journaling, or asking for help, can stabilize you and help you stay grounded.*

- **Remember why you started**: Reflect on the pain addiction caused and the freedom you now have from it. *Write it down. Speak it out loud. Keep a photo, journal entry, or reminder nearby. Recovery is a choice you keep making—not because it's easy, but because it's worth it.*

- **Expect setbacks, not perfection**: Recovery isn't a linear process. There will be moments of struggle, but struggle is not failure. *Resilience is built in the rebound. Every time you respond to difficulty with courage and grace, you grow stronger.*

Use tools, not willpower: Journaling, mindfulness, CBT strategies, values reminders, grounding exercises—lean on the skills you've learned. *You don't have to "tough it out." You have tools now. Let them work for you.*

A Final Message of Encouragement

Every day you stay in recovery is a victory. Some days will be easier than others, and some will stretch you in ways you never expected—but the most important thing is to keep moving forward, one choice, one moment, one breath at a time.

You are not just sober, you are thriving, healing, and becoming the person you were always meant to be. Recovery is not about erasing the past—it's about building a future rooted in courage, compassion, and clarity.

You have already proven your strength by taking the first step. And you will continue to grow, not despite your challenges, but because of how you rise through them.

**Keep going. You are worth it.
You are enough. You are not alone. And your story is far from over.**

FOR SOMEONE WHO HAS A LOVED ONE STRUGGLING WITH ADDICTION

Loving Someone with an Addiction is Painful—But You Are Not Alone

If someone you care about is struggling with addiction, many emotions come into play. First and foremost, I want you to know that all your feelings are valid. The anger, the frustration, the sadness, the hope, and the heartbreak—these are all justifiable feelings. It is essential to know that you are not alone in this and that there are ways to find support for yourself.

Loving someone with an addiction is one of the hardest things a person can go through. You want to help, but you do not know how. You want them to get better, but you cannot force them. You are tired, worried, and scared of what the future holds. But there is hope, and there are ways to support your loved one while also taking care of yourself.

Understanding Addiction as a Disease, Not a Choice

It is easy to think, "Why can't they just stop?" or "If they loved me, they would change." But addiction is not simply about willpower; it is a complex disease that affects the brain, decision-making, and behavior. Recognizing this truth is a crucial step in transitioning from anger and frustration to compassion and support.

Addiction is not a reflection of your loved one's love for you. It does not mean they are weak or selfish. It means they are struggling with something that requires professional support and, most importantly, their own willingness to recover.

Supporting Without Enabling

One of the most challenging aspects of loving someone with an addiction is figuring out how to help without enabling. Enabling means unintentionally making it easier for them to continue their addiction. Some common enabling behaviors include:

- Giving them money (which may be used for substances)

- Covering up for their actions or making excuses

- Bailing them out of legal or financial trouble

- Putting their needs before your own well-being

- Instead, healthy support looks like:

- Encouraging them to seek professional help

- Setting firm and loving boundaries

- Not shielding them from the consequences of their actions

- Seeking support for yourself through therapy, Al-Anon, or NAMI groups

Setting Boundaries with Love

Boundaries are essential—not just for your loved one but for you. Setting boundaries does not mean you do not care. It means you love them enough to protect yourself while encouraging them to take responsibility for their recovery.

Examples of healthy boundaries:

- "I love you, but I will not give you money for drugs or alcohol."

- "I am here to support you, but I will not lie or cover for you."

- "I will help you find treatment, but I will not rescue you from the consequences of your actions."

Caring for Yourself While Supporting Someone in Addiction

You cannot pour from an empty cup. Loving someone in addiction can take a significant toll on your mental, emotional, and even physical well-being. Taking care of yourself is not selfish; it is necessary.

Ways to Care for Yourself

- **Seek support**: Groups like Al-Anon, Nar-Anon, and Families Anonymous are specifically designed for family members and loved ones of individuals struggling with addiction. These groups offer a safe, nonjudgmental space for individuals to share their experiences, receive support, and learn practical coping strategies. They help families understand the nature of addiction, set healthy boundaries, and begin healing their own emotional wounds, which are caused by fear, stress, and chaos addiction can bring into the home. Perhaps most importantly, they remind families they are not alone. Connecting with others who truly understand what you're going through can be a powerful source of comfort, clarity, and hope. You don't have to carry this burden by yourself.

- **Consider therapy:** You deserve a space where your feelings are heard and validated. Therapy can help you process complex emotions like guilt, anger, sadness, or helplessness—feelings that often come with loving someone who struggles with addiction. A skilled therapist can also guide you in setting boundaries, rebuilding trust, and reclaiming your own sense of peace. Whether it's individual, couples, or family therapy, this space is yours for healing, growth, and perspective.

- **Engage in self-care**: Caring for yourself is not selfish; it's essential. Recovery affects the entire family system, and your emotional well-being is important as well. Try to find time for things that refill your cup, such as exercise, mindfulness, journaling, creative hobbies, reading, connecting with others, or simply resting. The goal isn't perfection—it's balance. Small acts of self-care remind you that your needs matter and that healing happens one moment at a time.

Letting Go of Guilt and Understanding Their Journey

It is not your fault. Say that again: It is not your fault. You did not cause this, and you cannot cure it. The only person who can honestly decide to recover is the person struggling with addiction. Your job is not to fix them—it is to love them in a way that encourages healing and accountability.

Sometimes, despite all your efforts, your loved one may not be ready for change. That is not a reflection of your love or your efforts. Recovery happens on their timeline, not yours. The best thing you can do is support them without losing yourself in the process.

Hope for the Future

Addiction is a dark road, but recovery is possible. Millions of people have found their way back, and your loved one can too. While you cannot walk the path for them, you can be a steady presence of support and love—without compromising your own well-being.

There is hope. For them. For you. For your relationship. Keep holding onto that hope and never hesitate to seek help for yourself along the way.

Healing doesn't happen all at once, but it does happen—and every step forward matters. Even when things feel uncertain, your presence, your boundaries, and your willingness to grow can plant seeds of change. Keep going. You're not alone.

KEY TAKEAWAYS

Recovery is Possible for Everyone

I know this not only from the stories in this book, but also from my own experience. No matter how far someone has fallen, recovery can happen. If you're reading this and doubting yourself, please hear me when I say: there is always a way forward. Hope can emerge even from the darkest places.

There is No One Path to Healing

My recovery didn't look exactly like anyone else's, and yours doesn't have to either. Some people thrive in 12-step programs; others find strength in therapy, spirituality, or harm reduction. What matters is finding what works for *you* and permitting yourself to walk your own path.

Shame is the Enemy of Growth

I know shame all too well, and I also know that it kept me stuck longer than anything else. Addiction feeds on silence and secrecy. Recovery begins when we take a risk, speak our truth, and let others see the real us. It's scary, but it's also where freedom starts.

Connection is Essential

Addiction isolates; recovery connects. For me, connection came through people who told me the truth, loved me enough to hold me accountable, and reminded me I mattered. However you find it, support groups, therapy, friends, or family, connection keeps us grounded.

Lived Experience is a Valuable Form of Expertise

I may be a psychologist, but my most profound lessons didn't come from textbooks. They came from struggling, failing, and slowly finding my way back. The contributors in this book share that same lived wisdom. Their survival is their credential, and their words are proof that recovery is real.

Healing is Nonlinear, but Always Worth It

Relapses, setbacks, and pain are part of many recovery journeys, including my own. Healing doesn't move in a straight line, but every time we get back up, we grow stronger. What matters isn't perfection, but persistence.

Everyone Deserves a Second Chance (or a Third, or a Fourth...)

I've been given chances I didn't think I deserved, and I am grateful every day for the people who didn't give up on me. Nobody should be defined by their lowest moments. With compassion and support, people can and do change.

Family and Loved Ones Need Support Too

Addiction affects not only the person who is using, but also everyone who loves them. Families deserve to heal and care for themselves just as much as individuals do. I've seen how powerful it can be when loved ones get their own support, and how that ripples back into the recovery process.

Recovery is About More Than Abstinence

Sobriety alone isn't enough. True recovery is about building a life worth living—one filled with purpose, relationships, joy, and integrity. It's about waking up with peace of mind and the freedom to be yourself again.

You Are Not Alone

I can't stress this enough: you don't have to do this by yourself. I once believed I was beyond help. I wasn't, and neither are you. Some people will walk this road with you if you reach out your hand.

Stories Have the Power to Heal

Sharing our stories chips away at stigma and shame. It builds bridges and gives others the courage to speak up too. The stories in this book, and maybe one day yours, are reminders that honesty heals not only us but the people who hear it.

Recovery Requires Ongoing Care and Commitment

Recovery isn't something you graduate from. It's something you practice, like tending a fire that needs fuel every day. Meetings, therapy, spiritual practices, service, connection; these are the logs that keep it burning. The good news is, the longer you tend it, the stronger and brighter it becomes.

A Note from Dr. Mac

If you're holding this book right now, I want you to hear me clearly: recovery is possible. I don't just say that as a psychologist; I say it as someone in long-term recovery who has walked through the shame, the cravings, and the doubts. I know what it feels like to think you can't change, and I also know the joy of realizing you actually can.

I hope that these stories, tools, and resources remind you that you are not broken, you are not alone, and you are worth fighting for. You don't have to have it all figured out. You just need to take the next step, and then the one after that. Keep going. You matter.

RESOURCES AND MENTAL HEALTH SUPPORTS

This list is designed to support you—wherever you are on your journey. Whether you're seeking help for yourself, a loved one, or exploring the world of recovery, these resources offer connection, healing, and hope.

It reflects what has helped me personally, what I recommend to clients, and what others have told me has made a meaningful impact on their lives.

🪨 Crisis and Helpline Numbers

- National Suicide & Crisis Lifeline – Call or text 988
  24/7 free and confidential support for people in distress.
- SAMHSA" National Helpline – 1-800-662-HELP (4357)
  Substance Use and Mental Health Treatment Referral and Information. Available 24/7 in English and Spanish.
- Crisis Text Line – Text HOME to 741741
  Connect with a trained crisis counselor via text, 24/7.
- National Domestic Violence Hotline – 1-800-799-SAFE (7233)
  24/7 confidential support and safety planning.
- Trevor Project Lifeline – 1-866-488-7386 or Text START to 678678
  Crisis support for LGBTQ+ youth.

🏥 Treatment & Recovery Services

- SAMHSA Treatment Locator
  findtreatment.gov
  Search for nearby treatment facilities and programs.
- Partnership to End Addiction
  drugfree.org

Offers tools and guidance for families navigating substance use.

- Shatterproof
  shatterproof.org
  National nonprofit focused on transforming addiction treatment and ending stigma.
- Recovery Research Institute
  recoveryanswers.org
  Science-based addiction recovery research and education.
- The Phoenix – thephoenix.org – Free sober active community with fitness and social support.

12-Step and Peer Support Programs

- Alcoholics Anonymous (AA)
  aa.org
- Narcotics Anonymous (NA)
  na.org
- Al-Anon / Alateen – Support for families and teens
  al-anon.org
- SMART Recovery – Self-management and recovery training
  smartrecovery.org
- Celebrate Recovery – Christian-based recovery
  celebraterecovery.com
- Recovery Dharma – Mindfulness-based recovery
  recoverydharma.org
- Women for Sobriety – Support for women in recovery
  womenforsobriety.org
- In the Rooms –24/7 global online recovery meetings
- intherooms.com

Faith-Based Recovery Resources

- Celebrate Recovery – celebraterecovery.com
- The Salvation Army ARC – salvationarmyusa.org
- Faith Partners – faith-partners.org
- JACS (Jewish Alcoholics, Chemically Dependent Persons and Significant Others) – jacsweb.org
- Muslim Wellness Foundation – muslimwellness.com

Mental Health & Co-Occurring Support

- NAMI (National Alliance on Mental Illness)
  nami.org
  Education, support, and advocacy for individuals and families affected by mental illness.
- Mental Health America (MHA)
  mhanational.org
- The Jed Foundation
  jedfoundation.org
  Promoting emotional well-being and preventing suicide for teens and young adults.
- The Trevor Project (LGBTQ+ Youth)
- thetrevorproject.org
- RAINN – rainn.org – For survivors of sexual abuse and trauma
  rainn.org

Therapist and Support Directories

- Psychology Today – psychologytoday.com
- Open Path Collective – openpathcollective.org
- Therapy for Black Men – therapyforblackmen.org

- Therapy for Black Girls 🛡 – therapyforblackgirls.com
- Inclusive Therapists 🛡 🌀 – inclusivetherapists.com
- National Queer & Trans Therapists of Color Network 🌀 🛡
  – nqttcn.com
- Melanin and Mental Health 🛡 –
  melaninandmentalhealth.com
- 🌀 LGBTQ+ Specific Recovery & Mental Health Resources
- Pride Institute – pride-institute.com
- QTPoC Mental Health – qtpocmentalhealth.org
- Trevor Project – thetrevorproject.org
- National Queer & Trans Therapists of Color Network –
  nqttcn.com
- It Gets Better Project – itgetsbetter.org
- 🛡 BIPOC & Cultural Support
- Sista Afya – sistaafya.com
  Mental wellness and community care for Black women.
- Latinx Therapy – latinxtherapy.com
  Therapist directory, podcasts, and culturally responsive
  resources.
- Black Emotional and Mental Health Collective (BEAM) –
  beam.community
  Education, advocacy, and healing justice for Black
  communities.

Specialty & Niche Support Resources

These resources serve unique populations and offer specialized tools, support, and community. Whether you're navigating recovery within a specific cultural, legal, or life context, these organizations may meet your needs in meaningful ways.

US Veterans & Military

- Veterans Crisis Line – Call 988 then press 1 / Text 838255
  24/7 crisis support for veterans, service members, and their families.
- Give an Hour – giveanhour.org
  Free mental health services for military and veterans.
- Wounded Warrior Project – Project Odyssey –
  woundedwarriorproject.org
  Free retreat-based mental health programming for veterans living with PTSD and related challenges.

🎓 Youth & Collegiate Recovery

- Young People in Recovery (YPR) – youngpeopleinrecovery.org
  National network supporting youth and young adults in recovery.
- Association of Recovery in Higher Education (ARHE) –
  collegiaterecovery.org
  Supports collegiate recovery programs and campus peer networks.
- The Jed Foundation – jedfoundation.org
  Mental health advocacy and suicide prevention in schools and colleges.

Justice-Involved Individuals

- The Center for Justice Innovation – innovatingjustice.org
  Works to reduce incarceration through treatment-focused alternatives.
- Prison Yoga Project – prisonyoga.org
  Brings mindfulness and trauma-informed yoga to incarcerated populations.
- Lionheart Foundation – Houses of Healing – lionheart.org
  Emotional literacy and trauma recovery for people in prison

Recovery & Wellness Apps

Sobriety & Recovery Support

- I Am Sober – Sobriety tracking, daily pledges, and milestone reflections
- Sober Grid – Social networking and peer coaching for recovery
- Loosid – Sober social network with dating, events, and recovery groups
- Pocket Rehab – Anonymous, real-time chat-based peer support and crisis intervention
- Pear Reset – Personalized recovery support with daily check-ins and accountability tools
- Sober Time – Visualize your sobriety time, track goals, and read motivational quotes
- Nomo – Sobriety Clocks – Track your sobriety with multiple clocks and motivational badges
- SoberTool – Daily motivational messages, relapse prevention tools, and sobriety rewards
- WEconnect Health – Build healthy routines, track recovery activities, access virtual support

- In the Rooms – 24/7 online recovery meetings and a global community for multiple pathways
- 12 Step Companion – A portable toolkit with the Big Book, prayers, promises, and recovery tools
- My Spiritual Toolkit – Daily recovery readings, gratitude journal, and 10th step inventory tool
- AA Big Book Free – Mobile version of the AA Big Book, including prayers and personal stories
- SMART Recovery CBA – Cost-Benefit Analysis tool to weigh the pros and cons of behaviors and choices
- The Voyage – Personalized addiction recovery app offering coaching, support, and self-guided tools

Meeting Finders

Meeting Guide – Official AA app that helps you find in-person and virtual AA meetings
Pink Cloud – Meeting locator, sobriety tracker, and space for step work notes

Mindfulness and Meditation Apps

- Insight Timer – Free guided meditations, sleep, and mindfulness tools
- Twenty-Four Hours a Day – Daily meditations and reflections for people in recovery
- Aura – Personalized meditations, stories, and life coaching tools
- Shine – Mindfulness for BIPOC and underserved communities; daily self-care support
- Mindful – Meditation practices and mental wellness tools from Mindful magazine

- 12 Step Meditations – Guided meditations aligned with 12-step principles
- Buddhify – On-the-go meditations organized by what you're doing or feeling
- Balance – Personalized meditation plans that adjust with your feedback
- Soothing Pod – Sleep meditations, bedtime stories, and calming music

Journaling and Reflection Apps

- Tangerine – Daily habit tracker and mood-based journaling with customizable prompts
- Day One – Award-winning journaling app with photos, reminders, and secure syncing
- Reflectly – AI-driven journal designed to boost positivity and help process emotions
- Journey – Guided journaling with prompts for gratitude, goal setting, and mindfulness
- Diarium – Journal that integrates with your calendar, social media, and health data
- Gratitude – Simple app focused on daily gratitude journaling and affirmations
- Moodnotes – Combines journaling with CBT-based tools to help improve thought patterns
- DailyBean – Cute and colorful journaling focused on mood and micro reflections
- Zinnia Journal & Planner – Visual journal with templates, stickers, and self-care logs

- Penzu – Private, secure online journaling with encryption and custom templates
- Stoic. – Combines journaling, reflection, and stoic philosophy for emotional resilience

Mental Health Support Apps

- eMoods – Mood tracking designed for individuals with bipolar disorder
- MoodLog – Track moods, symptoms, medications, and triggers
- Moodpath (now MindDoc) – Mood journal and mental health screening tool for depression and anxiety
- Moodtrack Social Diary – Real-time mood tracking with optional anonymous social sharing
- Daylio Journal – Mood tracker and micro-diary with fun, visual charts
- CBT Thought Diary – Identify cognitive distortions and challenge negative thinking patterns
- Remente – Mood tracking, goal setting, and mental wellness coaching in one
- Wysa: Mental Health Support – AI chatbot for emotional support, plus human coach options
- HealthfulChat – Mental health peer chat rooms with topics including addiction and recovery
- 7 Cups – Free, anonymous emotional support with trained active listeners and therapists
- DailyStrength – Online support groups for a wide range of mental and emotional health issues

- Psych Central – A hub of articles, tools, and moderated support communities for mental health
- Motivate – Daily motivational videos and affirmations to energize and inspire
- ThinkUp – Personalized affirmations with voice recording and habit tracking
- My Affirmations – Simple app for positive self-talk with reminders and categories
- What's Up? – Combines CBT and ACT techniques to help with anxiety, anger, and stress
- AntiStress – Interactive tools and games to manage anxiety and release tension
- Medisafe – Medication reminder app with visual pill tracking, alerts, and adherence logs
- BPHope.com – Companion to bp Magazine with articles, strategies, and community support
- Focused – Journaling and life tracking specifically designed for individuals with bipolar disorder

Sleep and Relaxation Apps

- Headspace – Guided meditations, sleepcasts, and breathing exercises to wind down and reduce stress
- Calm – Sleep stories, soothing music, guided meditations, and calming visuals
- Pzizz – Uses psychoacoustic science to help you fall asleep, nap, and stay focused
- Slumber – Sleep-inducing stories, meditations, and soundscapes tailored for better rest
- Sleep Cycle – Smart alarm and sleep tracker that analyzes your sleep patterns and wakes you gently

- Noisli – Custom background sound combinations to enhance focus, relaxation, or sleep
- 10% Happier – Meditation app featuring sleep content and calming talks from renowned teachers
- Moshi – Sleep and mindfulness app designed for children, with bedtime stories and meditations

📖 Books, Podcasts & Media

Books:
- *The Unexpected Joy of Being Sober* by Catherine Gray
- *Cognitive Behavior Therapy: Basics and Beyond (3rd)* by Judy Beck
- *Rewired: A Bold New Approach to Addiction and Recovery* by Erica Spiegelman
- *This Naked Mind: Control Alcohol, Find Freedom, Discover Happiness & Change Your Life* by Annie Grace
- *Breathe: The New Science of a Lost Art* by James Nestor
- *You Will Get Through This: A Mental Health Tool Kit- Help for Depression, Anxiety, Grief, and More* by Julie Radico, Nicole Helverson, and Charity O'Reilly
- *In the Realm of Hungry Ghosts* by Gabor Maté
- *Automatic Habits* by James Clear
- *The Gifts of Imperfection* by Brené Brown
- *A Gentle Path Through the Twelve Steps: The Classic Guide for All People in the Process of Recovery* by Patrick Carnes
- *Beyond Addiction: How Science and Kindness Help People Change* by Jeffrey Foote, Carrie Wilkens, and Nicole Kosanke
- *Refuge Recovery: A Buddhist Path to Recovering from Addiction* by Noah Levine
- *DBT Skills Training Manual* by Marsha Linehan
- *Empowering Your Sober Self: The LifeRing Approach to Addiction* by Martin Nicolaus

- *No Bad Parts: Healing Trauma and Restoring Wholeness with the Internal Family Systems Model* by Richard Schwartz
- *Eye Movement Desensitization and Reprocessing (EMDR) therapy: Basic Principles, protocols, and procedures (3rd edition)* by Francine Shapiro
- *Self-Compassion: Stop Beating Yourself Up and Leave Insecurity Behind* by Kristin Neff
- *The Anxious Generation* by Jonathan Haidt
- *Codependent No More: How to Stop Controlling Others and Start Caring for Yourself* by Melody Beattie
- *I Am Not Sick: I Don't Need Help! How to Help Someone Accept Treatment* by Xavier Amador
- *Loving Someone in Recovery: The Answers You Need When Your Partner Is Recovering from Addiction* by Beverly Berg
- *It Takes a Family: A Cooperative Approach to Lasting Sobriety* by Debra Jay
- *Understanding and Helping an Addict: A Guide for the Family* by Andrew Proulx
- *Don' Let Your Kids Kill You: A Guide for Parents of Drug and Alcohol Addicted Children* by Charles Rubin
- *Addictive Thinking: Understanding Self-Deception* by Abraham Twerski
- *The Lost Years: Surviving a Mother and Daughter's Worst Nightmare* by Kristina Wandzilak and Constance Curry
- *Man's Search for Meaning* by Viktor E. Frankl
- *The Four Agreements: A Practical Guide to Personal Freedom* by Don Miguel Ruiz
- *The Recovery Book* by Al J. Mooney, Catherine Dold, and Howard Eisenberg
- *Addiction Recovery Management: Theory, Research, and Practice* by John F. Kelly and William L. White
- *Chasing the Scream: The First and Last Days of the War on Drugs* by Johann Hari
- *Let Them* by Mel Robbins

- *The Body Keeps the Score: Brain, Mind, and Body in the Healing of Trauma* by Bessel Van Der Kolk
- *The Practicing Happiness workbook: How mindfulness can free you from 4 psychological traps that keep you stressed, anxious, and depressed* by Ruth Baer
- *Untamed* by Glennon Doyle
- *Straight Up* by Trent Shelton
- *Girl, Wash Your Face* by Rachel Hollis
- *Girl, Stop Apologizing* by Rachel Hollis
- *Forgiving What You Can't Forget* by Lysa Terkeurst
- *Why Has Nobody Told Me This Before?* by Julie Smith
- *Lost Connections by* Johann Hari
- *Chasing the Scream* by Johann Hari
- *Stash: My Life in Hiding* by Laura Cathcart Robbins
- *Unsung Heroes: Deconstructing Suicide Through Stories of Triumph* by Kristie Knights
- *Dopamine Nation: Finding Balance in the Age of Indulgence* by Dr. Anna Lembke
- *Stop Doing that Shi*t* by Gary John Bishop
- *Unfu*k Yourself* by Gary John Bishop
- *Wise as Fu*k* by Gary John Bishop
- *The Gift of Forgiveness* by Katherine Schwarzenegger Pratt
- *The Myth of Normal: Trauma, Illness, and Healing in a Toxic Culture* by Gabor Maté with Daniel Maté
- *The Subtle Art of Not Giving a F*ck* by Mark Manson
- *Everything is F*cked: A Book About Hope* by Mark Manson
- *Beautiful Boy: A Father's Journey Through His Son's Addiction* by David Sheff
- *Clean: Overcoming Addiction and Ending America's Greatest Tragedy* by David Sheff
- *Tweak: Growing Up on Methamphetamines* by Nic Sheff
- *We All Fall Down: Living with Addiction* by Nic Sheff
- *High: Everything You Want to Know About Drugs, Alcohol, and Addiction* by Nic Sheff
- *Think Again by Adam Grant*

- *You Are Not Alone by Ken Duckworth*
- *It's Ok That You're Not OK by Megan Devine*
- *Don't Feed the Monkey Mind by Jennifer Shannon*
- *Alcohol Explained 2 by William Porter*
- *Celebrate Recovery* by Rick Warren and John Baker
- *Celebrate Recovery Inside* by John Baker

Podcasts:
- *The Bubble Hour*
- *Sober Powered*
- *Recovery Elevator*
- *The Naked Mind Podcast*
- *The Hello Someday Podcast*
- *The SHAIR Podcast*
- *The One Day at a Time Podcast*
- *The Way Out Podcast*
- *The Rational Egoist*
- *The Sobriety Diaries*
- *Clean and Sober Podcast*
- *Addiction Unlimited*
- *Therapy Chat*
- *Unlocking Us with Brené Brown*
- *The Trauma Therapist Podcast*
- *The Hardcore Self Help Podcast*
- *The Happiness Lab with Dr. Laurie Santos*
- *Where Should We Begin? With Esther Perel*
- *Hopestream*
- *The Family Recovery Solution*
- *Love Over Addiction*
- *Elevate Your Life with Jenell Riesner*
- *Ten Percent Happier with Dan Harris*
- *The Rich Roll Podcast*
- *Armchair Expert with Dax Shepard*
- *On Being with Krista Tippett*

The world of recovery and mental health is always growing. If you find a resource that helps you or someone you love, write it down. Keep your own recovery toolkit evolving.

REFERENCES

Alcoholics Anonymous. (2001). *Alcoholics Anonymous: The story of how many thousands of men and women have recovered from alcoholism.* (4th ed.). Alcoholics Anonymous World Services.

Baer, R. A. (2014). *The practicing happiness workbook: how mindfulness can free you from the 4 psychological traps that keep you stressed, anxious, and depressed.* New Harbinger Publications, Inc.

Baker, J. (2021). *Celebrate Recovery Leader's Guide, Updated Edition.* Harper Christian Resources.

Beattie, M. (2022). *Codependent No More: How to Stop Controlling Others and Start Caring for Yourself.* Spiegel and Grau.

Beck, J. S. (2020). *Cognitive behavior therapy: Basics and beyond* (3rd ed.). The Guilford Press.

Carl Rogers. (2012). *Client Centered Therapy (New Ed).* Constable & Robinson.

Celebrate Recovery Homepage. (n.d.). Www.celebraterecovery.com. Retrieved July 19, 2024, from https://www.celebraterecovery.com

Levine, N. (2014). *Refuge Recovery.* Harper Collins.

Linehan, M. M. (2015). *DBT Skills Training Manual* (2nd ed.). Guilford Publications.

Marlatt, A., & Donovan, D. (2008). *Relapse prevention: maintenance strategies in the treatment of addictive behaviors.* Guilford.

Miller, W. R., & Rollnick, S. (2023). *Motivational Interviewing: Helping People Change and Grow* (4th ed.). Guilford Press.

National Alliance on Mental Illness. (2025). *Support and education for individuals and families affected by mental illness.* Retrieved from https://www.nami.org

Neff, K. (2015). *Self-compassion: stop beating yourself up and leave insecurity behind.* William Morrow.

Nicolaus, M. (2017). *Empowering Your Sober Self: The LifeRing Approach to Addiction Recovery* (2nd ed.). Lifering Press.

Recovery Dharma. (2025). *Recovery Dharma: How to use Buddhist practices and principles to heal the suffering of addiction.* Retrieved from https://recoverydharma.org

Schwartz, R. C. (2021). *No bad parts: Healing trauma and restoring wholeness with the internal family systems model.* Sounds True.

Shapiro, F. (2018). *Eye movement desensitization and reprocessing (EMDR) therapy: Basic principles, protocols, and procedures* (3rd ed.). The Guilford Press.

SMART Recovery. (2025). *Self-Management and Recovery Training.* Retrieved from https://www.smartrecovery.org

Substance Abuse and Mental Health Services Administration. (2025). *Substance use treatment and recovery services.* Retrieved from https://www.samhsa.gov

The Phoenix. (2025). *Sober active community.* Retrieved from https://thephoenix.org

van der Kolk, B. (2015). *The Body Keeps the score: Brain, mind, and Body in the Healing of Trauma.* Penguin Books.

Volkow, N. D., Koob, G. F., & McLellan, A. T. (2016). Neurobiologic Advances from the Brain Disease Model of Addiction. *New England Journal of Medicine, 374*(4), 363–371. https://doi.org/10.1056/nejmra1511480

Women for Sobriety. (2025). *Helping women overcome alcoholism and other addictions.* Retrieved from https://womenforsobriety.org

World Service Office. (2008). *Narcotics Anonymous.* Narcotics Anonymous World Services